The Attention-Deficit

WORKPLACE

The Attention-Deficit

WORKPLACE

Winning Strategies for Success in
Today's Fast-Paced Business Environment

Mitch Thrower

Edited and with an Introduction by
Bill Katovsky

The Lyons Press
Guilford, Connecticut

An imprint of The Globe Pequot Press

To buy books in quantity for corporate use
or incentives, call **(800) 962–0973, ext. 4551,**
or e-mail **premiums@GlobePequot.com.**

The Lyons Press is an imprint of The Globe Pequot Press

10 9 8 7 6 5 4 3 2 1

Printed in the United States of America

Designed by Sheryl P. Kober

ISBN 1-59228-612-7

Library of Congress Cataloging-in-Publication Data is available on file.

BEFORE MY DAD passed away in 1999 at the age of 89, we spent several weeks going through his photo albums. After looking at one photo from World War II that showed him surrounded by cheerful French children after the U.S. Army liberated their bombed-out village, I asked him what advice he would he give his grandson, if one day I'm blessed to have a son. He thought for a minute, then said, "Live. Be sure to live while you're here."

For all the advice, for all the love, for all the opportunities, and for telling me to go get a job when I asked you if I could borrow $10,000 to start my first company, this book is dedicated to you, Dad.

TABLE OF CONTENTS

Introduction: Achieving Success on the Run, by Bill Katovsky   **xi**

Welcome to the Attention-Deficit Workplace   **xix**

The Attention Law of 100   **1**

The Real ATM—Your Attention Time Machine   **3**

The Toggler   **5**

Hold on to the Handlebars, or, Some Calls Can Wait   **7**

Whack the Right Moles   **9**

Pay Attention to the Details of Communication   **11**

Position Yourself at the Right Place at the Right Time   **12**

The Incredible Shrinking Employee   **13**

Think Big, Think Creatively   **14**

Never Send a Forward, Unless . . .   **16**

"I See Spam People"   **18**

The Billon-Dollar Secret Weapon Is Humor   **21**

The Hawaii Ironman   **23**

Jacqueline Kennedy's Personal Touch—Old School Is New School   **26**

Be My Guest   **28**

The Global Virtual Desk—Instant Messaging   **30**

Fake Happiness Won't Fly   **32**

Be a Good Listener   **34**

The Driving Force   **35**

Pull Up a Chair   **37**

Get an Assistant   **39**

The Perfect Business Model   **41**

Throw Away Your To-Do List and Start Over   **44**

Surround Yourself and Your Office with Clocks   **45**

The Term Sheet   **47**

The Yule Log—Simplicity and Creativity Often Achieve
the Best Results   **50**

Cutting-Edge Technologies that Will Save You Time
and Attention   **53**

Weapons of Mass Distraction: Hidden Agendas   **55**

Star in Your Own Reality Television Show   **57**

The Bunker-Busters: Come Out with Your Money!   **59**

You've Got S-Mail!   **61**

Learning the Dance of Avoiding Capture in Conflict   **63**

The Delivery Room   **66**

Do-Over, or the Power of a Repeat Performance   **68**

Managing Up   **71**

Getting Your Résumé Noticed   **74**

TGIF—Thank God it's Friday   **77**

Multitasking   **78**

"The Smartest Guys Win"   **80**

Winning Food Strategies **85**

The Art of Negotiation Doesn't Have to be the Art of War **88**

Deadlines—Greet and Meet Them **92**

Home Office Alone? **94**

Aligning Your Interests **97**

The Office Divide: Create vs. Implement **99**

Sharing Ideas with Others **101**

Focus, Focus, Focus **103**

Back Up Your Files, Back Up Your Files **105**

Repeat Offender **107**

The Founder's Dilemma **109**

Password Amnesia **113**

Going Legal **115**

The Office Romance **117**

Get it in Writing **121**

The Ten-Second Rule **123**

You've Been Googled! **125**

Practice the Art of Storytelling **127**

Pay Attention to Yourself: Top Ten Personal-Needs Checklist **129**

The 59th Lesson **131**

Acknowledgments **135**

{INTRODUCTION}

Achieving Success on the Run

BY BILL KATOVSKY

WE'RE ALL FAMILIAR with the Attention-Deficit Workplace. Its whirlwind energy sucks us into its dizzying orbit. We feel powerless against information and time-demands bombarding us from every direction. We lose our bearings in the fast-paced tumult. Our attention wanders. We grow bleary and bloated from data glut. Due to time constraints, decisions are made on the fly, or not at all. Projects get postponed or abandoned. Meetings are interrupted. Personal relationships are strained. Even our health takes a beating.

Yet we can't place life on hold, or press the *delete* key on management or co-workers. We need to discover new strategies in coping with diminished productivity, while toppling all those attention-deficit barriers that stand in our way.

Today's office has become hyperactive and inattentive. Underneath the fluorescent lights hums the ceaseless murmur of restlessness and discontent caused by stress. It's an affliction caused by attention-deficit disorder, or A.D.D. But this kind of A.D.D. doesn't refer to a person. *It's our entire frenzied business culture that suffers from A.D.D.*

The modern office shares many of the same characteristics as an adult person with A.D.D. (or clinically referred to as A.D.H.D.—attention-deficit hyperactivity disorder—and represents about 5 percent of the adult population). If you are in denial about your own unhealthy work environment, ask yourself: do these attention-deficit symptoms occur in your workplace?

✓ Is your office disorganized?

✓ Does your workplace often get distracted by new projects that never get completed?

✓ Is the pace of work too hectic?

✓ Is everyone running late for appointments and meetings?

✓ Are deadlines always being pushed back, or not even met?

✓ Are projects shuffled aside or delayed indefinitely?

✓ Is office morale often at low ebb?

✓ Do co-workers frequently seem bored and listless?

✓ Is there a lack of motivation and self-initiative?

✓ Is office productivity hampered by co-workers spending too much time on personal matters?

✓ Does it seem that no one *really* listens?

✓ Is faulty, ineffective multitasking used as a convenient excuse for lack of focus?

If you answered yes to any of the above symptoms, then your office experiences A.D.D., which affects how and where you work. We can easily assume that a whopping majority of businesses suffer from A.D.D. An epidemic? Absolutely.

We chuckle at the cubicle culture wonderfully satirized in *Dilbert*. We read best-selling time-management books like Kenneth Blanchard's *The One Minute Manager*. We attend management seminars. We go on company weekend retreats to air our grievances, strategize, and find solutions to chronic interpersonal difficulties. We set our watches ten minutes ahead. And yet, we are losing the war in the Attention-Deficit Workplace. It is a war fought on two overlapping fronts: time and attention.

We have all this great technology at our disposal to enhance the speed of communication, but we have lost the ability to communicate simply and effectively with one another. In the supercharged work environment, we often feel that no one is listening; no one is paying 100 percent attention. We grow frustrated and exasperated by our daily immersion in this toxic-technology work environment.

Because we are all on the clock, time must somehow be managed. We live in a 24/7 world that beeps, rings, pings, and chirps with cell phones, BlackBerrys, Instant Messenger, e-mailing, and pagers. Time is our most precious and limited commodity, especially in a world of short-attention spans. The clock keeps ticking, indifferent to our needs as daily distractions continue to increase.

The Attention-Deficit Workplace wasn't created by globalization, cell phones, and the Internet. These factors only made the problem more apparent by speeding up the pace and tempo of the workplace, while adding additional webs and layers of information to keep track of and process. Does this mean that more things get accomplished? Or do the limited resources of time, attention, and money get further stretched, often past the breaking point?

So what should be done?

For starters, read *Attention-Deficit Workplace* by my friend Mitch Thrower. It will show you how to prosper and thrive in today's business culture. The book is both a diagnosis of the Attention-Deficit Workplace and a prescription for a sane, healthy recovery from this modern ailment affecting most employers and employees.

—◊◊◊—

"He can't ever sit still." "He's constantly in motion." "He's the human hummingbird." I've used each of these descriptions to describe Mitch Thrower. He's high-energy, with an impressive entrepreneurial track record. He's built companies from scratch and sold them at handsome profits. He's courted venture capitalists. Now he's applied his business skills to a phenomenon we can all relate to in our time-crunched, information-overload world.

The *Attention-Deficit Workplace* is based primarily on Mitch's business experiences. It's also sprinkled with some stories from his parents. He grew up in the upscale town of Westport, Connecticut. His mother, Lori, was one of Jacqueline Kennedy's executive assistants in the early 1960s. His father, Fred, was a television pioneer right before and after WWII, and later became president of a large New York City television station where he created the holiday viewing staple, *The Yule Log*. Mitch is 37 years old, with light brown hair and brown eyes, lean, athletic, square-jawed, and model handsome. He's a walking advertisement for Ralph Lauren apparel.

I met Mitch ten years ago when he was running a student travel business out of his two-story, glass-walled penthouse apartment in the seaside village of La Jolla, California, which is about ten miles north of San Diego. Looking out from the apartment's balcony, one could see downtown La Jolla fronted by a row of palm trees that were supposedly the inspiration for Dr. Seuss's tall fuzzy creatures (the late, real Dr. Seuss—Theodor Seuss Geisel—was a long-time resident of La Jolla). Mitch's living and working situation was as zany and chaotic as any Dr. Seuss story. A revolving cast of college interns were stationed in various rooms of the Mitch compound. They kept his travel business functioning, while his friends from the East Coast were always visiting, often staying for weeks at a time.

Apart from overseeing the travel business that was based on selling Eurail passes to American college students heading off to Europe for summer vacation or study-abroad programs, Mitch attended business school at University of San Diego for his MBA. He was also training for long-distance triathlons. A typical day for Mitch would involve an hour swim at the pool on the University of California campus, or in the La Jolla cove that was home to a small flotilla of noisy sunbathing seals. He'd then rush to school for classes or back to the apartment to supervise the interns. Several times a week, he'd go off on a three-hour bike ride through the hilly horse country of eastern San Diego County. His nights were filled with restaurants, parties (young, beautiful women pursued him like catnip), workouts at the gym, or a 10-mile run along the Pacific coast. His day usually culminated past midnight at the local 24-hour Von's, where he'd top off his shopping cart with a carboholic's assortment of MetRx energy bars, Honey Nut cereal, skim milk, orange juice, pasta, and tomato sauce.

In time, as our friendship blossomed, I watched with astonishment as he was able to compress more and more activities into his day. I would walk into his La Jolla bedroom-office, and there he would be standing by his desk in his running shorts and Nike tank top, checking his e-mail, talking to someone on a cordless phone, while wearing a headset for fielding incoming students' calls who were inquiring about purchasing Eurail passes, and, oh yeah, occasionally he would be wielding a dust rag or sponge in his free hand, usually cleaning something. When Mitch and I later went into business together, which involved a complicated buy-back of a sports magazine that I had founded, he was not only able to round up additional investors, but he began seriously training for the Hawaii Ironman. I often wondered how he found enough hours to prepare for an athletic endurance event as physically taxing as the Hawaii Ironman—a 2.4-mile swim, 112-mile bike ride and 26.2-mile run. I used to joke, "Mitch probably trains in his sleep." Throughout this nonstop, hectic period, he also profitably arranged the sale of his student travel business.

Not only did Mitch finish his third Hawaii Ironman in Kona in 1997, he did so in a highly respectable time of around 11 hours, which placed him in the top quarter of the field, many of whom train more than 20 hours per week. With all the time demands placed on him, Mitch still managed to perform at the top of his game amidst some of the world's fittest athletes.

In the years since, Mitch expanded his business horizons by becoming a successful web entrepreneur when he launched an online event registration site for runners and triathletes with former business partner Scott Kyle. Racegate.com was naturally housed in a spare bedroom. It started with one paid employee—a part-time student from Brazil who had come to San Diego to train for triathlons and spoke with a heavy Portuguese accent on the phone to race directors scattered all over the United States. Mitch met him at the pool. Within two years, the site grew exponentially, handling online transactions for dozens of participatory sports. Fueling its growth was an expanded management structure and a sea of money that flowed in from venture capital funding. Following a merger with its main competitor, Racegate acquired a new name, Active, and web address, *www.active.com*. The company now employs more than 300 in a swank San Diego office building.

With a keen, roaming eye for challenge mated to business opportunity, Mitch began looking abroad for new endeavors. He launched a European-based software company founded on the same business model as Active—online athletic event participation—with the intention of capturing market share in countries such as South Africa, France, England, Germany, and Italy. Mitch was now spending half the year in southern France where he set up a new office in Aix-en-Provence. Whenever he returned to La Jolla, he would lecture once a week at University of San Diego's business school as its "entrepreneur-in-residence." He also maintained his seat on the board of directors at *Triathlete* magazine where he writes a popular monthly column. He has started—and finished—13 Ironman races, always ranking in the top of his age group. And he's not slowing down—in sport, in life, in business. In addition to training for the 2004 Hawaii Ironman, he negotiated the sale of Active Europe to Active.

While observing my friend in action, I'd quip, "Life's a Mitch," since he simply refused to let distractions—time, people, events, or circumstances—slow him down, put him in a foul mood, or derail his plans. To label him an optimist is an understatement. Nor is he the type of boss or leader who bullies others to get ahead. He's a gentleman at all times. Never a rude word, never a cross remark. He leads and inspires by encouragement, not discouragement. He's all carrot; there's no stick in his dealings with others. Mitch represents the opposite of the dog-eat-dog combativeness celebrated on business reality television shows. Sorry, but nice guys can finish *first*. But to finish first, today's entrepreneur, executive, or manager must know how to effectively navigate the business world's time and attention maze.

The always-in-motion Mitch is ideally situated—professionally and personally—to write about operating efficiently in the eye of the hurricane. Now he's sharing his insights, experiences, practices, and strategies in *The Attention-Deficit Workplace*. This book will help eliminate time and attention deficits from your own life. It's packed with useful parables, observations, and real-life scenarios that address today's business culture. You will find chapters dealing with business growth, improving efficiency, teamwork, setting priorities, staffing, management, co-workers, and investor relations. More important, following each parable is a brief lesson that will help you improve your own time and attention management.

Now is the time to regain control of your life within the workplace. Give your career the attention it deserves. Use this book as a starting point—and good luck!

Bill Katovsky is the founder of Tri-Athlete Magazine, *and co-author of* Embedded: The Media at War in Iraq *(The Lyons Press), which was awarded Harvard's Goldsmith Prize for best trade book in 2003 on media, politics, and public policy.*

Welcome to the Attention-Deficit Workplace

OUR BUSINESS CULTURE is ruled by short attention spans and time-gulping demands. While interest payments on the U.S. budget deficit averages several billion dollars a day, a much heavier burden of debt currently affects businesses: it's the runaway deficit of time and attention.

In these pages, you'll learn that someone wasting your time is far worse than someone wasting your money. You can always make more money. Time, on the other hand, is a limited asset that diminishes daily. In every workplace interaction, in every business meeting, in every profit forecast or spreadsheet, the units most often missing, misunderstood, or mismanaged are time-related.

The Attention-Deficit Workplace will help you address the critical and neglected aspects of time and attention in today's business culture, which is locked into permanent fast-forward. You might not be able to control what your competition does, but you have control over how you spend time at work and you have the power to give your job the full attention it deserves.

This book is my up-close-and-personal examination of what happens inside our business culture as it becomes increasingly dysfunctional with A.D.D. What are the warning signs? What are the causes and symptoms? How can they be prevented? Why should we care? And what can we learn?

This book will help you balance your time and attention budget. Many of these parables are grounded in stories from my own experiences as a serial entrepreneur working in the trenches building several software, marketing, and commerce businesses. So think of this book as my personal guided tour through the time and attention labyrinth.

Now, how should you read the *Attention-Deficit Workplace*? Start anywhere you want. Skip around at your discretion as your time or attention dictates.

All the best,

Mitch Thrower
April 2005
La Jolla, California

PS: Please e-mail me if you'd like to share your own time- and attention-deficit stories, solutions, and lessons for inclusion in future volumes in the *Attention-Deficit Workplace* book series. I look forward to hearing from you.

Mitch@AttentionDeficitWorkplace.com

Or visit the website and sign up for the free Attention-Deficit Workplace Newsletter, and post your thoughts or experiences at *www.Attention DeficitWorkplace.com*.

The Attention Law of 100

IN 2001 THERE were 3,645 people listed in my address book. Then I made the decision to follow my Attention Law of 100. This law states that you can only really know 100 people. And once you hit 101, you should delete someone. I mean it. It took a ruthless application of the *delete* key to slim down to 100.

Think about it. Who is on your speed dial? Who is programmed into your mobile phone? Should they be there? If you want to know who's high on your priority list, check your phone records. It might just shock you. If 100 sounds like too few for your address book, just ask yourself this question: When did you call or connect with the people you think might make your list of 100 contacts? It would take you 100 days, or just over three months, for you to call just one important contact per day.

Your attention is your ultimate yet limited resource; it's far better to invest it in a close 100 than a distant 1,000. A good test: If you were in Mexico, and got pulled over by some unscrupulous police officers and needed $10,500 to pay the traffic fine on the spot or go directly to jail, who would you call? My guess is that you know a maximum of three people who could help you out.

We are spread too thin in the Attention-Deficit Workplace. The problem is compounded by the ease with which people can meet someone new, add a contact to their phone book or database, and get an e-mail address. Now this, of course, depends on what kind of work you are in. I'm not talking about extensive PR lists or e-mail databases—you will also need those. I'm talking about the people you know and work with, and even the people you want to know and work with. There is no reason to be rude, but there are many reasons to limit the number of people you "know."

✓ **LESSON:** Every year, if your business address book is larger than 100 people, trim it. It should only contain the people in your life who truly mean something to you from a career and personal perspective. Create your own all-star team of contacts; don't be afraid to cut from the roster. The quality of your relationships will only strengthen. Invest your attention with the people who matter most.

The Real ATM—Your Attention Time Machine

FORGET THE CASH-DISPENSING ATM. The real ATM is your Attention Time Machine. We are constantly making withdrawals and deposits from this ATM. That is why you need to be aware of those time bandits who are always present in the workplace. These time thieves love to steal our time with something distracting or worthless.

My ATM problem hit me like a frozen halibut in London's Heathrow airport. After purchasing a cheese sandwich and coffee, I headed into the lavatory while I was on my cell phone, trying to hang up on a talkative ad salesman from France. As I looked up and caught an image of myself in the wall mirror, with my cell phone in one hand, my sandwich and coffee in the other hand, chewing, talking, and holding the *mute* button down to cover up the sound of flushing toilets in the background, I realized that I was in the feverish grip of a self-induced whirlwind.

On another occasion, I can remember missing an important business call when getting ready in the morning; it was from a curt, short-tempered executive in London and he made it very clear that because I was not available, he was not interested in my proposal. The next day, I installed a speakerphone in my shower and, every few months, I have to replace it.

✓ **LESSON: The quick-tempo nature of today's work environment requires a never-ending attention juggling act. It is one played by executives worldwide who must learn to handle all those electronic balls in the air. The most powerful concept we have to grasp is that attention and time are more valuable than any diamond. They are the most valuable things on earth. And yet, many of us are going to** bed at night with an attention-deficit account that's compounding interest daily. Some executives I know are so far behind on their time payments to the right constituencies, team members, board members, and shareholders that they don't know where to start, and so they find themselves hiding behind an electronic wall of impersonal e-mail, issuing electronic orders as if from an underground bunker. With the daily withdrawals and deposits of your attention, make sure your own ATM is not overdrawn.

The Toggler

ONE VERY RAINY Los Angeles morning, I found myself in the offices of a large media group, where I watched in silent amazement as a secretary deftly toggled between several screens on her computer. One screen featured a game of solitaire, another was a music-downloading program, the third involved a frenzied instant messenger chat with a friend, and the last screen showed a spreadsheet that she clicked on whenever a co-worker stopped by her desk. Her cell phone rang occasionally, and she would whisper something then hang up. Her behavior reminded me of those toggle switches you find at Radio Shack. She was a classic Toggler.

Togglers are everywhere. They are driving the SUV in front of you in rush-hour traffic, juggling a cup of coffee, changing a CD, speaking on their cell phone, checking their hair in the rearview mirror, and probably not paying much attention to the road.

You have probably been introduced to a Toggler at an evening business reception. This Toggler is simultaneously shaking your hand, sipping champagne, eyeing the food platter that's circling nearby, and looking over your shoulder to see if there's someone else more important to chat with.

Yes, Togglers are everywhere. They have learned to hyperlink life itself—opening and closing experiential windows at eyeball-distracting speed. Are Togglers more productive as a result of their hyperactivity? You be the judge.

In my estimation, Togglers are constantly in motion, but they seldom seem to be going anywhere. They have difficulty concentrating on one project at a time. As a result, their productivity suffers in a big way. In Paris, I've seen people in offices chat for hours in meaningless conversations on their cell phones while browsing websites. I always thought that the workplace is called the workplace for a reason, and

I'm fairly sure it has something to do with working. Telling that to a Toggler is, well, like explaining something to a cranky toddler. And we know how restless and easily distracted children are.

✓ **LESSON: You can toggle between people or projects, but you need to realistically assess what you are toggling between. Ask yourself if there is not a layer of unnecessary distractions in your toggling. Toggling is a poor excuse for multitasking when few of these tasks ever get satisfactorily completed.**

Hold on to the Handlebars, or, Some Calls Can Wait

WHEN YOU'RE BUSY and people need you, they often expect to be able to find you immediately, and this responsibility contains a powerful attraction. In the heat of Racegate's initial growth phase, I began to take my cell phone with me on bike rides and answer calls, until one day I hit a bump. Literally. Traveling down the long and steep Torrey Pines grade on the Pacific Coast Highway in Del Mar, California, my cell phone rang. In a moment absent of logic and rationality, I took my left hand off the handlebar and reached around for my cell in my jersey and answered the call. With cars rushing by, I said, "This is Mitch." and I heard a woman say "Mr. Throw—" and I hit a bump. I started to lose control of the bike, and the something-bad-is-about-to-happen slow-motion effect began. I had to grab the handlebars with both hands, and the first thing to do was let go of the cell phone. I could hear it crash into the middle of the road as I regained control of the bike and my composure.

I stopped my bike, with my heart pounding like a jackhammer. I turned and looked up the hill to see my poor little phone in the middle of the road, with cars racing over it. It was flipped open, a wounded creature. I ran towards it like an owner rushing to a stricken pet. One of the last vehicles to pass was a semi, and my Motorola V60i actually started to spin from the draft created by the truck racing past. After the 18-wheeler passed, I grabbed the phone. The craziest thing? When I picked up the phone I simply put it to my ear, and said, "Hello?" half-expecting to cut a deal with someone on the dead phone. It had gone that far.

That night, replaying the incident in my mind, I vowed to take my cell phone only for emergencies on bike rides. But it was not long before I figured out a way to clamp my cell phone to my handlebars so the caller ID could show, and if an important call came in, I could always pull off to the side of the road to field the call. My 24/7 mobile-attention behavior had almost cost me my life. I foolishly thought I had to answer every call. But the reality is I didn't.

✓ **LESSON: We can push our connectedness beyond sane and healthy limits. Too many people feel they must interact with others any time and any place, interrupting whatever people are focused on. Do not be afraid to turn off the ringer on your phone, or better yet, turn your phone off entirely for two full days per week. See how you operate with no cell phone two days out of every week. Hold on to the handlebars in and around your life—let go of the phone. (A friend calls cell phones "selfish phones.") Let go of your connection to other people for just a little while. See how it feels. A part of being connected is understanding how to identify and remove the nonessential.**

Whack the Right Moles

LET'S FACE IT: e-mail correspondence is the "Whack-the-Mole" game for attention-starved times. In this popular amusement park game, you have to hit every mole that pops its head up with a mallet, and the winner gets to bring home a $1.39 stuffed animal that will soon be thrown away.

The euphemism is apt. For many people, receiving messages still symbolizes hope. Every once in a while, a phone call, letter, or an e-mail message brings welcoming news, an exciting opportunity, or new work project. Receiving e-mail, once all the spam is deleted or ignored, strikes a positive neural chord that goes all the way back to the snail-mail age, when we would dig through bills to find a handwritten card or note from a friend, lover, or family member.

I know some people who are slaves to their e-mails. They have to read, sort, file, and reply to everything. They are prisoners of their in-box. What makes matters worse is that these same people tend to click the "opt in" boxes during online shopping and they subscribe to multiple newsletters. Incoming e-mail then spirals out of control. I think I realized what the word "inundation" meant in 2003 when I fell asleep with my laptop in bed. As my eyes started to close, I thought I was dreaming. I groggily could hear my e-mail management program chime every time an e-mail came in. Every few seconds, it chimed. Then, like popcorn in the microwave, the chimes of arriving e-mails became a popping flurry. I actually had to turn off the sound on my e-mail program because of the sonic inundation from inbound e-mails. It was then that I realized my e-mails were popping up faster than I could eat them.

When we allow this irrational "I have to reply to all messages immediately" mind-set to take over, messages become distractions. The routine of receiving and replying takes us away from more important tasks. This happens in every office, up to the highest executive ranks.

✓ **LESSON:** In this age of total accessibility, if you drop everything every time someone tries to reach you, you will find yourself doing more dropping than carrying. Don't connect with everyone, or with just anyone, all the time. The bottom line: Whack only the right moles and only during the most appropriate times. Create a correspondence strategy for yourself. Mentally define what you are trying to achieve with the people you are interacting with on a daily basis and then develop a routine that allows you to maximize useful contact and minimize unnecessary contact. Pick designated times for reading and replying to e-mails. Send terse but polite replies to unimportant messages from important contacts. If a message requires a lengthy response, pick up the phone instead. Get in the habit of completing tasks before you make or receive phone calls or e-mail messages. Remember that the only prize for having an empty in-box, and for sending responses to everyone who contacted you, is a few minutes of quiet. And, if you're lucky, a $1.39 stuffed animal.

Pay Attention to the Details of Communication

ONE OF MY FRIENDS had a girlfriend with a Hotmail e-mail account. He set up a new e-mail account and the name he selected was an exact duplicate of her name except with one letter missing. He then sent an e-mail to another person with whom he suspected she was having an affair. He simply sent one sentence on her behalf, "Hey Richard, my computer just crashed and I deleted all your e-mails from the past year, so can you send me them because I want to keep them?" Guess what happened? Sure enough, what came back in the e-mail was heartbreaking electronic documentation that confirmed his suspicions that she had been unfaithful.

With instant messaging and e-mail, the game of intentional mistaken identity looms large over both the work and personal landscape. I met a venture capitalist whose company did not have the exact web address that his company's name would logically own, and he said that the other "Frank" at the company, who actually owned the web address, was receiving tons of unsolicited business plans. The VC's response: "Good. I could never read them all, anyway."

✓ **LESSON: When someone contacts you for the first time, always confirm it is indeed the person he or she claims to be. And always be very careful of the *reply* button, because some e-mail programs make it easy to confuse *"reply"* with *"reply all."***

Position Yourself at the Right Place at the Right Time

IN 1999, I attended a speech at a technology conference in Los Angeles to hear a presentation from John Pleasants, a commanding and charismatic guy who was the newly appointed president of Ticketmaster Online City Search. I was in the process of growing my online company, Racegate, with the mission of becoming the "Ticketmaster of participatory sports." I waited until after his speech, then I scoped out the hall's exits, and which door he would be exiting from. I positioned myself in front of the right exit, and when he started to leave, I introduced myself in the doorway. With both my feet firmly planted, he would have had to physically go through me to get by. I wasn't moving until he heard my pitch on why Ticketmaster's next big growth market should be participatory sports.

After a 15-minute pitch, we shook hands and exchanged business cards. Ten minutes after I got in the car, John called me. "Mitch, I've been thinking about what you said, and I'd like to have breakfast with you tomorrow. Are you available?" Two months later, Ticketmaster invested millions with my company.

✓ **LESSON: Remember that the people you want to meet are just people and people need to eat, go to the gym, and speak at conferences. Executives around the world too often ride the roller-coaster of chance in interaction with others. Life will always have an element of random encounters. But when it's important to you, you need to point yourself in the direction of the people you need to meet. You have the capacity to do anything and everything in your power to meet whomever you want. Just be smart about it. Block the exit.**

The Incredible Shrinking Employee

WE ALL KNOW drab people who seem to just fade into the background. They are cursed by fate with a lifeless personality, a monotone voice, or worse, a voice that just happens to match precisely the background chatter in a crowded room. It's difficult to pay attention to these colorless people. There was one such team member at Active.com, whom I'll call Tony. He arrived at the company with one of the mergers, and whenever he wandered the halls and came around to the offices, people would pick up the phone and pretend they were busy. Tony was simply an impossible person to pay attention to. Sometimes when he was talking, I would find myself drifting off and watching his mouth move just like a foreign movie, only without subtitles.

Tony was ultimately terminated because he could not figure out how to get anyone's attention. He was easy to downsize because he was already invisible. He was a nonentity. And once, when I actually asked him detailed questions about a business issue, he had nothing to say.

✓ **LESSON: Be acutely aware of those people who have nothing to say. Don't be afraid to tell them that you have something else you have to do, or that you do not have time for them. We all have our charity cases that we give our time and attention to, but be realistic if someone is burning your time.**

Think Big, Think Creatively

THE FIRST COMPANY I started the day after I graduated from Saint Lawrence University was The College Connection. My mission was to help larger companies market their products and services to college students. In the early days of the business, it was only my best friend, Todd Adelman, and myself. We were faced with the necessary challenge of contacting large Fortune 500 companies and making them listen to our business pitch—how to market credit cards, phone cards, and Eurail passes to college students. It was like trying to scale Everest without Sherpas or oxygen tanks. Marketing folks at the larger companies rightly suspected that we were really just two young guys with a fax machine.

My dad always told me that if you wanted to get someone's attention, you should send them something that will not fit in any desk drawers, or the round filing cabinet in the corner (the trash can). So I created a large poster-board presentation that included an electronic pushbutton recorded message that was sent to a very senior American Express executive. His name was Ed Cooperman, and he was the COO of American Express. After I sent the oversized, techno-proposal to him, we waited by our single phone line and the silent fax machine. And we waited. After two long anguish-filled weeks, the phone rang. I answered, "College Connection, this is Mitch," and a deep demanding voice said, "What on earth is it?" I said, "How can I help you?" He replied, "This is Ed Cooperman over at American Express, and I've been having the hardest time trying to figure out what on earth this torn-up poster with wires is doing on my desk. It seems the folks downstairs in security thought it was a bomb, and they took it apart before they delivered it." He laughed as I explained to him what it really was, and that we wanted to promote American Express Cards to students accepted into study-abroad programs. Ed took a deep breath, and then said, "Bravo, I'll walk this down to College Marketing and tell them to make something happen with it." Three weeks later we had our first signed contract. American Express was our client.

✓ **LESSON:** In sending an unsolicited proposal to a company, you have to think big, and you have to be bold. Mapping your way through the labyrinth of a large organization to the right decision maker can be daunting. When in doubt, send your correspondence to the highest-ranking executive, with the understanding that he will likely send it to another department. There is a big difference between something that comes to a marketing department via the CEO and something that comes from an outside party with no internal connection. Use the internal corporate structure and its hierarchical dynamics to your advantage.

Never Send a Forward, Unless . . .

WHEN YOU KNOW that everyone's mailbox is filled with between 20 and 50 spam e-mails a day, who in his or her right mind would forward a joke or a rumor to anyone, especially a top executive?

Often people overlook the fact that many forwards are false—or based on urban myths. The website *www.snopes.com* tracks these urban myths. To see how prolific a forward is, you can also simply cut a sentence from any forward and type it in quotes in Google; you can then follow the links to its origins as an urban legend.

A few valuable forwards do make it into our e-mail boxes. But if they have made it to your in-box, they have likely made it into everyone else's. When people see your name on the "From" field in their e-mail box, they are identifying you with what they receive. Spammers also use forwarded e-mail strings filled with people that "CC" everyone or put everyone in the "To" field to mine the e-mails for valid e-mail addresses for later spamming. It's the time-tested power of association, and indeed you are associated with the voice, the context, and the content of what you forward.

If you want people to take you seriously, then be yourself, be original, and be brief. Some of the most effective communication is the one-word reply. John Pleasants, the president and CEO of Ticketmaster, is a master of the one-word reply. He'll reply to lengthy proposals with words like "Strong," "Weak," or "Call." If the proposal is really good, he'll "CC" someone who can make the project happen, and say, "Let's do this."

✓ **LESSON: The simple rule: Make yourself and your words a rare commodity. And when you do communicate, be brief. If you want to** send someone something funny, then write it in your own words, no matter how long it takes. In today's busy world, less communication is definitely more—especially electronically. In addition, using your own original text in an e-mail to someone accomplishes a very important goal. You're already sending a note through thin air to someone—you might as well let those words be yours.

"I See Spam People"

IN THE SPINE-TINGLING movie, *The Sixth Sense*, Haley Joel Osment plays a small frightened boy who, with bold and teary eyes, whispers to Bruce Willis, "I see dead people." Blessed (or cursed) with supernatural powers, he was capable of seeing and communicating with dead people who wanted him to solve their problems, so they made themselves visible to him.

I almost felt like that child actor one afternoon at the office. I had ducked into the rest room to avoid someone who consistently wasted my time at work. I leaned towards the mirror, shut my eyes, and breathed heavily against it, causing it to fog up. I then opened my eyes wide, and said in a joking fashion, *"I see spam people."*

You can set up junk filters on your e-mail, but spam still muscles its way into your in-box. And it's the same with certain kinds of undesirables in the workplace. You want to delete these people from your work life without resorting to rudeness or cruelty. You want these spammers to vanish.

You know who they are.

Circling the conference room like a bird of prey is the **High-Maintenance Investor** who wants to be involved in every part of your business because he invested $3,000 in the firm's very first round of financing. This is probably his first investment, but he considers himself as financially astute as Bill Gates.

In the company kitchen you find the **Billiard Shot** who is a college fraternity pal of the CEO, but never gets anything done, and ricochets from project to project in a futile attempt to prove himself to the organization.

In the hallway outside your door or cubicle, **The Talker** gabs endlessly because he or she grew up with nine siblings. This person will chatter nonstop, from nine to five. Plug your ears or invest in headphones if you don't like hearing about wedding and birth announcements, baby showers, weekend ski trips, or holidays in Cabo.

Lurking throughout the building or office is **The Stalker** who is convinced that a solid personal relationship with you in the workplace will advance his or her career, and is always presenting you with a "hot new idea" that has probably been cribbed from the *Bottom Line* newsletter.

What should you do about that particularly annoying creature known as **The Buzzword**? Find the nearest flyswatter. Almost every sentence he or she utters is packed tightly with tech talk or consultant speak. They love using words like bandwidth, paradigm, robust, synergy. Ask The Buzzword if a project is done, and instead of receiving a simple yes or no answer, you get this jargon-murky reply: "I didn't have the required bandwidth today to find a scalable solution so I will repurpose . . ."

Nor can we hope to sidestep **The Complainer** who wanders around the office like a sheriff without a badge, horse, gun, or posse. He is always complaining about others at work or how HR has unjustly allocated his paid time-off. He complains when the coffee pot runs dry, but don't ever expect him to replenish it with fresh brew.

The Tempest likes to hover near your desk, just waiting to create a conflict between you and someone else in the company, or to spread gossip because it makes him or her feel important.

When you are about to call it a day, you'll need to find a way to somehow sneak past **The Hallway Monitor** who likes to stand in the middle of the hallway, saying to you at 6:00 P.M. as you are rushing to get to the gym, "Can I talk to you for a sec before you leave?"

These are the spam people. You want to avoid them. It's like a game of dodge ball. You need to dodge, duck, dip, and dive from their unwanted presence. They rob you of your time. They want your attention. They have little sense of boundaries. All you want to do is tell them to scram.

✓ **LESSON:** The best way to manage these unwanted spam people is to set firm guidelines on your time. You might even have to employ advanced strategies to avoid them so you can be productive. For example, you may want to work at your computer wearing headphones (this is called "going under") or use a phone headset. When someone tries to talk with you, just hold up one finger and point to your ear, as you randomly say "Yes, yes" into the headset. As an emergency back-up plan, you may want to have a code that you can instant message to a friend, which will immediately trigger a phone call so you can really say, "I have to take this call." And don't forget to always build an exit plan into the start of any conversation at work, something like, "I've only got fifteen minutes, so let's try to accomplish everything you need to in that time frame."

The Billon-Dollar Secret Weapon Is Humor

THE IMPORTANCE OF laughter in managing your business relationships is often neglected. This is a mistake. By knowing how to make people laugh, you open yourself to spending time with friends and laughing so hard you can barely breathe. In the early '60s, my dad liked going to New York's trendy 21 Club with his friend, Charlie King, who liked to drink and laugh. According to my dad, Charlie was a big fella. When Charlie told stories at the bar, my dad would laugh so hard tears came to his eyes. And as Charlie laughed along with him, everyone around them wanted to know what was going on.

Dad recalled one occasion when Charlie, unhappy about someone's curious ears at the bar, walked over to the eavesdropper. With a big smile on his face, Charlie reached his arms out and gave the man a big bear hug. It was a hug so tight that the man could not move. In the full grip of his hug, Charlie picked the man up, and carried him to the door and simply said, "I think you'll be going now." Dad was bent over the bar, still laughing. He loved to spend time with Charlie, but knew that Charlie was having a tough time in business. His good humor was masking his personal pain. He was a salesman with a great sense of humor, but he was not selling anything.

Dad knew that Charlie possessed the right personality for natural success, but lacked the jumpstart necessary to get his big break. So Dad, who was the president at WPIX-TV in New York, had a simple idea that he discussed with Charlie over dinner. The idea was for Charlie to try to secure the rights to a show for his television station in New York and the tri-state market. Dad told Charlie that he would put $50,000 in escrow and if he was able to secure the rights to this show, Dad would give Charlie the $50,000. If Charlie secured the rights to other metropolitan markets, he would then own these other market rights as an incentive.

Charlie certainly proved his mettle as a salesman. From a little old German man, Charlie secured the rights to the *Our Gang* comedies, otherwise known as the *Little Rascals*, and received his $50,000. Charlie then started his own syndication company out of his kitchen in New Jersey and sold the *Our Gang* comedies in other markets. His company, which was called King World Enterprises, with the astounding management skills of Charlie's two sons, Michael and Roger, ultimately became one of the most successful syndication companies in the world. It was sold to CBS in 1999 for $1.8 billion.

✓ **LESSON: When you think about the people you know at work and in your personal life, you almost always remember the ones who are funny, and these are the people you want to be around. An essential ingredient in friendship is humor. One of the best-kept secrets of a sense of humor is to listen, because everyone has a different idea of what's funny. Some people love the movie *Office Space*; some people love Robin Williams; others prefer *Curb Your Enthusiasm*.**

The common mistake many executives and managers make is that they fall into critical humor—making fun of others. Respectful humor that supports others will open a new world of opportunities for you. Critical humor may solicit a laugh, but it will make others question whether you'll ridicule them when their backs are turned. Be funny, but be supportive.

The Hawaii Ironman

SOMETIMES ATHLETIC EVENTS seem bigger than life. Take, for example, the Hawaii Ironman. People all over the world design their lives around the quest to qualify for and participate in an Ironman. And not just in Kona, though the Ironman Triathlon World Championship on the big island of Hawaii is, of course, the big show. Anywhere in the world, a 2.4-mile swim, 112-mile bike, and 26.2-mile run can offer the challenge and excitement associated with achieving a lofty personal goal. There are people who would relinquish almost anything to do the Hawaii Ironman. I've met people who've given up their jobs, their cars, their homes, and ultimately their significant others for the opportunity to line up in the shallow waters of Kailua Bay with 1,600 of their closest triathlon friends. I've also met people who have enhanced their jobs and relationships thanks to Ironman.

I have a friend who was a first-time Ironman triathlete in 2004. Matt Landa, the president of The Active Network, once told me, "Training and preparation for an Ironman is all-encompassing; it bleeds into all your daily thoughts and actions. Ironman is an event that, once you decide to do it, you think about every day."

I agree with Matt. Once you decide to do an Ironman, everything you eat, everything you do, all the hours that you sleep, suddenly become hyper important. You begin to pay close attention to how you spend your time. You will find out exactly how much time you wasted at work. You'll discover the people in your life who drain your energy and those who recharge it. In training for an Ironman you'll find out what is important to you. In racing an Ironman, you'll build your self-confidence to an unimagined level.

Whenever I train seriously for the Hawaii Ironman, I wake up almost every night in a sweat. Not from nerves, but from my body burning whatever it needs to burn. I have yet to find an expert who knows why my body does this. But I know that when I have to change my shirt at 2 A.M. for weeks on end, I am in Ironman mode. Race night, I'll often wake up looking at my watch and planning to change my shirt. But for some reason it's always dry the night before the race—the calm before the storm.

If you've never been to Kona to watch the Ironman, you are missing a slice of life that NBC's coverage—though award-winning and inspiring—can never recreate. There is energy on the island, and the only way to really understand it is to call your travel agent and book a week's vacation in Kona, Hawaii. Watching the race live is guaranteed to have a profound impact on your life.

Becoming an Ironman is like putting an invisible self-confidence charm in your pocket. Whatever you do for the rest of your life that may seem difficult, you can pull out that charm and know that you can make it through anything.

Last summer, on a long bike ride to the mountain town of Julian, just east of San Diego, I was stalked and then passed by a super-fit woman with blond hair escaping from the vents in her helmet. I pedaled frantically to catch up, not so much for my ego, but in pursuit of some conversation. Acknowledging my effort, she slowed to a more reasonable pace, having already made her athletic statement. We started to talk, and I learned that, in a few weeks, she would be doing her second Ironman. When I told her that I was getting ready for my ninth Ironman, she looked at me through her Oakley sunglasses and said, "Mitch, what's your lifetime Ironman? Now that you know you can achieve great athletic things, what are you going to set your heart on that is non-athletic?" I could see the reflection of my image and the horizon in the silver lenses of her glasses, and I paused, still pedaling. "That's a good question," I responded, breathing heavily. She smiled. Descending the next hill, my new friend waved back at me and picked up the pace, appearing smaller and smaller as she moved away. She was leaving me behind to think, sweat, and understand her point.

✓ **LESSON:** This yellow brick road to Hawaii, or to any Ironman race worldwide, will be jammed with many valuable lessons. You'll learn that your bike shoes are like ice skates on the slippery floors of grocery stores and that a bike can seem just a few pounds lighter than your running shoes. You will also learn very difficult lessons that will shake and sort your priorities in life like a powerful earthquake, revealing the basic truths that support what and who is really important to you. If you're not too myopically focused on your training and equipment, then the Ironman just may teach you what you honestly value in your life. You will learn the basic lessons of what to eat, how to train, and how to run a marathon after being glued to your bike seat for more than 112 miles. You will learn that the wind, the rain, the heat, and the struggle are often overshadowed, even forgotten, when you reach the last few miles of an Ironman and find the courage to break through your own limitations.

The Hawaii Ironman Triathlon is also the ultimate attention-training exercise for well-conditioned athletes. It's an extreme example of balancing physical exercise with other priorities in your life. Even getting ready for a sprint triathlon or 10K, you have to fit training somehow and somewhere into your schedule. There are mental demons we fight and mental angels that we all carry around; it's how we deal with them that will determine if we can finish this thing called the Ironman, this thing called life.

Jacqueline Kennedy's Personal Touch—Old School Is New School

RESPONDING TO THE thousands of letters to Jacqueline Kennedy after the assassination of her husband was a resounding lesson and rewarding experience for my mom, Lori, who worked in Jackie's New York office as one of her executive assistants. Letters continued to pour in for years following JFK's murder; the entire world shared a love for JFK and for Jackie, and they reached out to her by sending letters of support. Jackie wanted to respond to every letter.

An entire room was filled with volunteers opening and sorting the mail and helping to respond to people around the world who had taken the time to write a letter or send gifts. Jackie's kindness was contagious and her thoughtfulness was evident in everything she did. She was always quick to send flowers or a thoughtful handwritten note to people she knew when they were going through good or challenging times.

When Jackie and my mom would ride home occasionally together up Park Avenue, driven by a Secret Service agent, they would reflect on the day and the people they were corresponding with and share humorous stories.

✓ **LESSON: In a world where a handwritten letter is an anomaly, attention to different forms of text has changed dramatically in the last decade. During the late '80s and early '90s when you wanted to get someone's attention, you would send them a fax. During the late '90s you would send an e-mail. Now, just after the turn of the century, the retro art of expressing thanks or congratulations or regret with a** handwritten note is the sure way to secure another's attention. Call it old school, but a handwritten note stands out among bills, e-mails, memos, and invoices. It's usually the first thing that you open on your way from the mailbox to your front door. It's the fun, unexpected surprise. In business, adding the personal touch will put you in a completely different category in someone's life. Even if it's hard to address everyone with a handwritten note, take the time to correspond on a personal level. Take your correspondence beyond the black-typed text not just by handwriting it, but by putting personality, genuine concern, and kindness into the note.

Be My Guest

THE ABSOLUTE BEST way to develop a relationship with someone that will lead to a powerful connection and meaningful interaction is to wake up with them. Perhaps not in the same bed, but under the same roof.

We've all heard of bedroom politics, or bedroom management. When two people are married or dating in an organization, smart people know that they likely share everything—and I mean every secret. It has also been said that a secret is something that you tell just one person—at a time. But the point I'm making is not about pillow talk, it's about the impact of intimacy. I have noticed the intimacy I've been able to develop with friends, training partners, or business partners by a) living in a nice place and by b) inviting them to stay in the guest room when they are in town. I remember when I invited an executive to come to La Jolla and he asked for a place to stay, I insisted he stay at my apartment, which he did. We got to have breakfast together. Let's face it, handing someone towels for them to use in the shower, and setting them up in a nice guest bedroom is an intimate interaction typically reserved for families.

Over the years, I've invited merger candidates, business partners, and potential employees to stay as house guests. When you are immersed in a living experience with someone, you are destined to develop a more lasting and personal relationship. It also establishes you as the host and captures the attention of your associates, because you control the playing field and consequently have their attention.

✓ **LESSON: Have a guest room. Make it more comfortable than the Four Seasons; have clean towels, a new bar of soap, privacy, a big table for people to spread their stuff out on, a place for someone to feel** comfortable and to experience your hospitality. Invite the people you want to do business with or work with into your home environment and it will improve the quality of your interaction and increase the depth of your relationships.

The Global Virtual Desk— Instant Messaging

BARRY DILLER, THE chairman and CEO of IAC/InterActiveCorp, stated that one of the great innovations to emerge from the Internet gold rush was the instant messenger application. I met the first investor and father of one of the founders of ICQ, the source of the instant messaging software, at a technology conference sponsored by the now-defunct publication *Industry Standard*. Yossi Vardi had 400 million green paper reasons to agree with Barry. But like all new time-consuming technologies, we have some catching up to do.

Should corporations allow instant messenger accounts on their employees' desktops? Is the instant messenger a distracting or an enabling technology? The first time I woke up to the power of instant messenging was when I was negotiating a multi-million dollar deal with America Online in 2001. I was on the phone with two individuals from AOL and I knew that both were in different geographic locations. I could hear them each typing, and suddenly realized that they were reacting to my comments; they were obviously communicating over the instant messenger with each other during the negotiation. Used this way, instant messenger is an advanced method for teleconference participants to gang up on one or more parties, to form communication alliances.

It is a powerful philosophical vision of the instant messenger that our entire network of friends and co-workers can be easily connected. We're all sitting together at a global virtual desk, with the capacity to reach out with a few keystrokes, and ask someone something.

✓ **LESSON:** While instant messenger technology allows us to know when someone else is logged in, there are downsides to this technology, especially when someone "types in your ear." It's hard not to respond, and it can serve as an attention and time vacuum cleaner that sucks you away from your work and your objectives. So, the simple solution? The words "Be right back." Just type them. People will almost always find something to do when you're not there, or engage in Internet conversation with others. So if you type, "Be right back," they will likely move on to another task or IM window.

Remember that all instant messenger conversations are logged and archived. As with your e-mail, don't ever type anything you don't want the world to someday see and easily attribute to you. Many things, when taken out of context, can be misconstrued. Many other things should never be permanently recorded.

Fake Happiness Won't Fly

ONE CAN'T FAULT Disney's Michael Eisner for feeling like one of the Seven Dwarves—Grumpy—after his highly publicized run-ins with board members and shareholders, which resulted in an early retirement timetable. But my own youthful experience working at Disney was far from stressful. I felt like another one of those dwarves—Happy.

In 1988, I was fortunate to have a summer internship at Orlando's Walt Disney World. Working at the theme park was a wish come true. From my childhood days vacationing there with my parents and sister Stacey, I always wondered why the entire world couldn't be more like Disney's. A youthful fantasy, perhaps partially realized, by moving later in life to La Jolla, California—another kind of magic kingdom.

As a new Disney team member (all team members are called "cast members"), I first had to graduate from Disney University, which is its corporate training program. I was indoctrinated with the Disney philosophy that's built around four core principles:

1. "Make Everyone's Dream Come True," in order to foster creativity.

2. "You Better Believe It," which considers the importance of product and service excellence.

3. "Never a Customer, Always a Guest," which means that a Disney theme park visitor is always referred to and treated as a guest.

4. "All for One and One for All," which focuses on the value of teamwork.

For my day job, I worked in River Country as part of Cast Services, which meant assisting vacationing families. Interacting with tourists from all over the country, you learn many things. To keep children from whining and losing interest, I would do magic tricks when it was raining. It's truly amazing how easy it is to convince a four-year-old that some object has disappeared.

My other work responsibility was clear across the park and required changing from the River Country costume, which was shorts and a T-shirt, into a navy pinstripe suit. In this suited role, I was able to meet with and learn from people in Participant Development, Conventions, and Cast Services. It is from these meetings with Disney executives that I learned something critical to my future success in business—that it is much easier for you to hold people's attention when you are genuinely happy. Not fake happy.

I was impressed by many things that summer. Disney knows how to put on a compelling show, and how to run a company. They know how to keep people's attention. Even more impressively, they know how to keep children's attention.

Walt Disney World is the theme park for the attention-deficit world. Just think about it, you can walk a few steps and move from Frontierland to Tomorrowland. Once you're inside the gates, all your senses are confronted with nonstop visual, auditory, and kinetic stimuli. This pleasing sensory bombardment from every direction is ideal in a family entertainment context. But finding this bombardment in the workplace, you'll end up feeling like Dopey if you can't filter out all the distractions.

✓ **LESSON: Children are perhaps the most natural attention barometers, because they will pay close attention to someone who is friendly, and they will often shy away from someone who is visibly distracted or grumpy. What I learned from Disney was not to be sleepy or grumpy, but to be happy. When interacting with others within your business environment, be happy, since this will encourage and inspire people to want to work with you.**

Be a Good Listener

I LEARNED THIS "attention-cement" technique from a close friend and a top executive recruiter, Scott Dunklee. As the CEO of La Jolla-based executive talent firm, The Lancer Group, Scott remembers and records what people are interested in. He's a world-class listener. If you've mentioned that you were following NASA's Mars Mission, or the progress of Jet Blue's stock, you'll soon find articles and clippings and e-mails on these topics, with an attached business card and a short note, checking in.

I've sat at business lunches with Scott and seen him in action with his conversational style of asking questions that translate into building interpersonal bonds. It's like a bricklayer pouring the cement foundation of human relationships. In corporate recruiting and in any dimension of business or life, listening and asking the right, relevant questions leads to a clear understanding.

Psychologists have a term for good listening technique. It's called "reflective listening," which acknowledges what someone else has said by repeating it back to the person, often with different words so as not to appear to be entirely an echo. This offers an effective way to build up trust quickly.

✓ **LESSON: One of the greatest human needs is to be heard. In the Attention-Deficit Workplace, people who listen are valuable, even priceless assets. Invest a little time and genuine support with real-world exchanges of information—grounded in what truly interests those in your world.**

The Driving Force

MY SISTER STACEY loved bunnies. She raised them while growing up. Dad would spend weekends building her hutches that looked more like the Four Seasons than rabbit cages for the little white and brown fluffy animals she so adored. Due to Mom's influence, she also loved gymnastics, reading, horses and life. She also loved listening to Rick Springfield. As teenagers, we took swimming lessons together at Longshore Club Park in Westport, Connecticut. She was beautiful, with a wise-beyond-her-years moral code, and she always knew what was right and what was wrong.

These childhood memories hovered just below the surface when, during a business school panel presentation to close to 100 people at The University of San Diego, someone in the audience asked me what motivates me to do so much—train for triathlons, teach at the university, become a serial entrepreneur. I paused to reply. Then, for the first time in my life, I uttered out loud these words, with a voice that was strong and clear: "When I was 14 years old, my sister died in my arms. She was 16."

The room went silent. My heart trembled. I waited a bit, then continued. "My sister Stacey had bone cancer that spread to her lungs. I was trying to resuscitate her, to help her breathe, but my CPR efforts weren't working. When your sister and best friend dies in your arms, something in your own mind short-circuits. Or rather, you suddenly become aware of new realities.

"For some, tragedy leaves them stuck in a pattern of prolonged sadness. For me, Stacey's death locked me on a different track. Through the sadness of loss and an acknowledgement of my own mortality, I found motivation and passion to live each day to its fullest.

"When life disappears in front of you, it's very big, and it's very real. I had to grow up pretty quickly after that. The loss of my sister set me on a course to make the most of this very short trip here on earth."

Glancing around the room, I saw faces looking back at me with understanding. And then, the oddest memory suddenly flashed before me: My sister and I were hiding beneath her bed during a thunderstorm when we were very young. As the sky boomed and shook with fury, she comforted me with these words: "Mitch, it's okay. Don't be afraid. The storm will pass. All storms do."

✓ **LESSON:** Wake up. You might have either a dream job or a nightmarish job. Either way, acknowledge where you are and who you are working with. If you're not content, rethink your priorities and ambitions. If you're wasting your time or your attention, then start investing it wisely. Your last day here could be tomorrow or it could be 50 years from now, but it will come. My sister Stacey gave me one of the greatest gifts of all: the gift of perspective.

Pull Up a Chair

MY DAD, FREDERICK Mitchell Thrower II, was born in 1910—decades before the birth of the television industry in which he would play a pioneering role. In the late spring of 1929, just before heading off to the University of Virginia to study medicine, he decided to visit New York City where he later got a telegram from his own father, Frederick Mitchell Thrower, who was in the real estate business in Tampa. (His father-in-law, Henry Snow, was the mayor there.) It said: "Son, about this college thing, send the money home. The banks just closed."

With this sudden reversal in his family fortune, my dad was forced to take a job with NBC Studios at their music library in New York. His job was filing records. But my dad was restless and he was an idea man. It was not long before he worked his way up through the managerial ranks to become the vice president of sales for the National Broadcasting Company. Later in life, he shared with me one of his innovative attention-grabbing techniques.

In the '30s, '40s, and '50s, it was traditional for executives to have big wooden desks with their chairs higher than those for guests. The implied power-trip objective was to make the executive feel a bit like a king and the visitor a loyal subject. Knowing that he would be at a positional disadvantage even before he walked into an executive's office to sell him advertising, Dad employed the following technique: Before each meeting, he would prepare a written proposal to help the executive understand how the client would generate sales. He would always walk into the office in a disarming manner, like a friendly, tail-wagging golden retriever. Before sitting down, he would grab one of those office chairs and carry it around the desk to the same side of the executive. With a smile, he would sit down next to the executive, and say, "Let's go over my proposal together, there are some things I want to point out." He told me that most people would respond favorably to the personal-space invasion, and would listen and learn from his proposal.

It's much easier to build a relationship of trust with someone when you are sitting on the same side of the table. When starting my businesses, I insisted that I have a round desk. This way, when someone comes in to talk with me or discuss an issue, we would sit together at the round table. There is a reason history does not tell the tale of the *Knights of the Square Table.*

✓ **LESSON:** Being on the same side of a desk or an issue is disarming, especially when discussing or analyzing a situation with someone. If you are on opposite sides of a desk, you will likely be on opposite sides of an issue. To capture someone's attention, you are required to look at the issue from that person's perspective. If possible, have a round desk and invite people to analyze challenges and solutions at your side.

Get an Assistant

MY FIRST ASSISTANT was Marne Berta. She worked with me in Westport, Connecticut for my first start-up, The College Connection Inc. She was a bright, motivated recent college graduate who, within a few weeks, demonstrated to me that my life was about to become a great deal more effective. She saw how overwhelmed I had become by starting this company from my apartment, so she would show up early every morning and tackle the tasks associated with managing the company. But she would also help with personal paperwork, insurance, even making travel arrangements, which, before online companies like Expedia, was a nightmare.

Marne said to me once, after I thanked her for going above and beyond the call of duty, acting at first as an executive assistant, then a personal assistant, then as the operations director for my life: "Mitch, I know that if you're trying to argue with an insurance agent, you're not doing what you need to be doing for the company. The more effective I make you, the more the company I'm working with will grow." Marne rocked.

Life is filled with things that simply must get done. We have to have car insurance, but we have no time to find the best one. We have to find out where we can take a class on Microsoft Publisher, but don't have time. We have to file things, make calls, and return things. There are all the things others expect us to do that fall into the monotonous chore category. It is amazing how exciting these mundane projects can be to someone who is actually getting paid by the hour to take care of them. Now if you don't have the budget for a full-time assistant, or if the office where you work is convinced that you still need to take out the trash and manage your own paperwork, then hire someone part-time and pay them out of your own salary. They can be a one-day-a-week person, a one-hour-a-day person, or even a once-a-month person.

Go through your to-do list, and identify how many things you could actually delegate to another person. Over time, your life and your business career will continue to hone your knowledge of what you need to do to be successful and avoid the interminable and multiplying minutiae that someone else should handle.

If you work in a corporation, it is critical to include professional and empowering assistants. This is not an area to cut for the budget. I can remember watching one of our top sales professionals at Active.com fight with a photocopier for almost an hour, when he should have been on the phone selling. If your work environment or corporate role does not afford you the opportunity to work with an assistant, hire a college student or an intern to help you on an as-needed basis. Until they sort it out scientifically, getting an assistant is one of the most effective ways to clone yourself, so you have the time to focus on the things you know you must do, with someone else handling the things that are necessary but distracting to you.

✓ **LESSON:** A personal assistant can alleviate stress in your life. I'm not talking about a spouse who takes care of the bills or a son or daughter who can mow the lawn. I'm talking about someone whom you can direct like an employee, and whom you can hold accountable. Someone to take care of what you know has to be taken care of but keeps getting postponed. How do you deal with things always left on the back burner? Not by staying in the kitchen. Find an assistant.

The Perfect Business Model

IN EARLY 1998, The Active Network began by selling online registrations to athletic events like the Bay to Breakers run in San Francisco and the Lavaman Triathlon in Kona, Hawaii. Within six years, *Inc.* named Active the 99th fastest growing private company in America. Active continues to expand globally, under the management dream team consisting of former West Pointer Dave Alberga, the disarming and highly skilled CEO with a pitch-perfect sense of humor; Matt Landa, the high school football star turned business pro; Jon Belmonte, the superb COO; and tech wizard Josh Schlesser—all under the watchful eagle eye of Kory Vossoughi, the-number-one-in-his-law-school-class corporate counsel. Active's management has successfully executed the formula of a winning business with reliable, renewable, and high-margin revenue streams. This is the same business model that supports Ticketmaster, Expedia, AARP, AAA, Moviefone, and Match.com.

Active reached this pinnacle of success as a world leader in the participatory sports world by adhering to what I call "The Perfect Business Model." There are hundreds of people who have played a significant role in the creation and the execution of Active's business model. But the first layer of the perfect business model is to build a business with reliable revenue.

Active made its revenue streams reliable by accepting the participant's cash first, before the athletic event director receives it. I remember what my dad once said: "The best way to make money is to help it move from one place to another and charge a fee." So that's what we did.

The second layer of the perfect business model is to have renewable revenue sources. Event directors put on triathlons and marathons every year. Little League administrators run leagues every year. People book swimming lessons at a national park every year. Fees are paid every year, over and over again. The industry of participatory sports is based on renewing flows of cash changing hands every year, every month, and sometimes even every day.

The third layer of the perfect business model is to have actual revenue. This may sound strange, but business models with identified sources of revenue were not always the norm. During the Internet bubble years of 1998 through early 2000, you would find businesses futilely chasing this illusory goal: "If we get people to sign on, we can figure out later how to make money from them." They greedily went after Internet eyeballs and venture capital dollars. In the end, they became virtual ghost towns. They failed because they were not dealing with reality. Because the Active business model was based on real, not phantom, multiple revenue streams from people, events, sponsors, and advertisers, it provided a stable platform for growth.

The fourth and most critical layer is one that often appears later in business models. This is an area I was always passionate about, at times forcing the company to pay attention to it, to take action on it, and to build these layers in the organization. The perfect business model must have a way to build in its own high-margin products that can be sold while processing reliable renewable revenue streams at any margin. For Active, one cash-cow product is the Active Advantage card, which is like a frequent-flyer membership card that offers discounts for travel and merchandise. The Active Advantage card offers healthy margins, while Active owns the reliable renewable transactions that present the higher margin membership product, along with useful messages from sponsors and advertisers. Active's current business expansion involves marketing and software services—additional green pastures filled with valuable cash cows.

✓ **LESSON: In most ventures, no single person can take credit for the enterprise. But in all enterprises, it's the business model that deserves detailed attention and understanding. At Active, I was one of the few people who saw the vision of Ticketmaster and the AAA** of participatory sports back in 1997 when the company's phone line was still in my name. Fueled by its success and venture investment, Active's business model, led by a dream team of skilled executives, is a now thriving enterprise having processed millions of dollars in transactions with the best software and technology available.

Throw Away Your To-Do List and Start Over

THE PLANE HAD just landed in Dulles from Paris. Following a successful meeting with the new team hired to launch my new web company, Active Europe, I was working on the plane for several hours before I fell asleep. As I dozed off, I slid my "urgent-things-to-take-care-of" folder filled with critical notes and phone numbers into the airline seat pocket next to the catalogue of merchandise and the United Airlines magazine. I had traveled for quite a while with that file, and guarded it closely. As you can guess, I got off the plane in a sleepy haze and left the folder behind.

I didn't realize it was missing until I landed at my final destination in San Diego. And you know what happened? Absolutely nothing. That's right; it had no impact on my work or personal life whatsoever. In fact, I barely even remember what was in that folder. In a way it was a reinvention of my to-do list. Our attention-deficit society loves lists—from David Letterman's Top Ten List to the list of groceries you're going to pick up after work. But it is ultimately the important things in our lives that we will remember, and every now and then it's a good idea to just start fresh with a new list.

✓ **LESSON: The first thing you should do with your to-do list today is throw it away. Start a new one. Whatever you remember from the first one deserves a place in your life.**

Surround Yourself and Your Office with Clocks

THE OPENING SCENE in *Back to the Future* takes place in Doc Brown's office, which is filled with clocks of all shapes and sizes. That scene was my inspiration to start collecting clocks, and I have clocks everywhere now. I have clocks in the shower, in the kitchen, displayed prominently in my car and at work. And I never set them ahead of real time. Setting your watch or clock ahead of time is the wrong way to get yourself to be on time.

The best way to be on time is to simply decide to be on time and to acknowledge that travel and meetings always take more time than originally anticipated. One of the great fallacies of time management is that setting clocks ahead of the accurate time encourages people to be early. A few years ago I found a clock that is so big that you can actually see the minute hand moving when you stand close to it. It's approximately four feet wide and four feet high, and it's striking. When I had it in my office, people would joke when they came past my office, asking, "Do you have the time?"

The question: "What time is it?" is answered by clocks. I have a 20-minute hourglass sand timer on my desk, and when I'm pressed for time, or getting ready to meet with someone who is a tad wordy, I'll tell them, "You have 100 percent of my attention for the next 20 minutes, but when the sand is not in the top of that hourglass, I have to go." It's amazing how efficient people become when they have limited time. It's like that the day before you leave for a vacation. For a year of my life, when I was traveling back and forth to our Paris office, I had that rushed, running-out-of-time feeling *all* the time. Because I always had an airline ticket with a departure date, I was forced to be efficient with my time. Plus, my Timex Ironman watch never left my right wrist. But it's easy to lose track of time when we're not surrounded by clocks or calendars. I have a giant calendar that outlines a full year in advance, and it's amazing how much smaller a year can seem when you make a calendar larger.

✓ **LESSON:** Surround yourself with clocks. To rule time you have to know how much time you are spending on what you are doing. The best way to do this is to put clocks in prominent places. Your life is not a Vegas casino, where there are intentionally no clocks, so it's easier for you to lose track of time. If you lose track of time, you lose time. Never set your watches just a few minutes ahead. It is a sure-fire way to always be just a few minutes behind.

If you're trying to get a seat in a restaurant or a Starbucks, here is a quick technique for inspiring people to leave their table if they're just lollygagging around. Ask them, or someone near them, in a nonthreatening way, "Excuse me, do you have the time?" They will then realize what time it is, and you need to reply, "Is it really that late already? Whew, this day is going so fast." This has an 80 percent success rate of inspiring them to move along—just make sure that your watch is not showing when you ask them, or your cell phone, which always displays the time. When people in your way have lost track of time, feel free to remind them.

The Term Sheet

IT'S LIKE BEING asked on a first date, experiencing your first kiss, or winning the lottery. This entrepreneurial moment is known as receiving what is called a "term sheet," which can be a several-page document from an investor who has decided that he would like to put capital in your venture.

Receiving a term sheet can be a wonderful, joyous, albeit frightening occasion. My first term sheet, in the spring of 1998, was, of course, more shocking to me than the feeling of locking lips with adorable Dara Liberson behind a gym locker in junior high school.

I had always built my previous business startups with a bootstrap mind-set, initially capitalizing them with credit cards and loans from friends. So, it was a fairly large shift of perspective to grasp the concept that one day the valuation of my new web venture for participatory athletes called Racegate—which, at the time, consisted of two guys and a business plan—would be worth $10 million. Racegate.com would now have $5 million in the bank, destined to be spent growing the business.

I am no longer a term-sheet virgin. My companies have received capital and offers in more than a dozen term sheets. And yet I have arrived at the conclusion that the entrepreneurial dating game with term-sheet wielding investors is fraught with hidden dangers, because your business is not worth much to you if you don't actually own it in the end. That means lawyers serve as critical keys to the adequate legal protection of your ownership.

Investor term sheets most often state that there will be a cash infusion into your business, and that you, the entrepreneur, must surrender something for that cash. Most often, it's equity. After years of negotiations with VCs and private investors, I've come up with the three life-saving laws for term sheets. These laws require you to pay close attention, or the romance will quickly sour.

1. *The law of 51 percent.* Pay close attention to your percentage of ownership, knowing that you may have to take in additional capital in the future. Fight to maintain 51 percent, or at least the voting control of whatever you are involved in. Losing 51 percent of a venture that you have built from the ground floor is like handing the keys to your house to a stranger.

2. *Make sure your lawyer is better than their lawyer.* And don't just base this comparison on their hourly rates either!

3. *Pay close attention to the term sheet's implications for your career.* You've heard of the golden parachute—which guarantees an executive a soft landing if he's let go. But in your negotiations with investors, if you lose 51 percent you should make sure to maintain the contractual right to be present at board meetings—even if it's just the right to observe.

In my experience raising money, I've also walked away from term sheets that were monkeyed up with terms that stripped away incentives. In Europe, I even received a term sheet from a company that was using another company's capital to invest, but was keeping the ownership equity for themselves. I did not walk away from that deal; I ran. If a term sheet is lacking integrity, it's likely that the investor is untrustworthy.

To the novice, term sheets may seem to read alike, but they are always distinct in their legalese. Term sheets can easily distract an organization by forcing everyone to keep their collective eyes off the ball—that is, running the business. Another pitfall that entrepreneurs must be aware of is that investors can drag out term-sheet negotiations until the business is desperate for cash. Then they can easily demand much, much better terms. When you can't make payroll, a term sheet from an outside investor becomes more compelling. The VCs can be cutthroat at this stage of a company's financing. If you push a VC for his aggressive reasoning, you might just get the hard-nosed answer, "Because I can."

It is well worth the effort and energy to spend the time to clearly understand the implications of every paragraph in a term sheet, because it can have an exponential impact on your future, and the future of the company. A term sheet is like a prenuptial agreement and a coach's playbook. Spend the time to understand the plays, and what happens should you ever separate from the business. Also, never be afraid to ask for more from an investor, or to stand firm demanding 51 percent of the voting stock.

✓ **LESSON:** When landing and negotiating a term sheet, spend the time to understand all of the implications. Investors have been doing this far longer than most entrepreneurs. Even slight nuances that appear in term sheets tend to address things far out into the future. In fact, the start-up entrepreneur might even be oblivious to what the future might have in store. A term sheet will be how you are financially graded, so you need to treat it with a far greater seriousness than your first romance. Study this map to your future. Be attentive to the details. Otherwise, the honeymoon won't last.

The Yule Log—Simplicity and Creativity Often Achieve the Best Results

BY THE TIME I was born in 1968, Dad had taken over as president of WPIX-TV Channel 11 in New York City. Television was a terrific creative outlet for him. He was always coming up with fresh ideas for news broadcasts, programming, advertising, and operations. He is perhaps best known for coming up with the idea for *The Yule Log*, a televised shot of burning logs filmed at the mayor's Gracie Mansion in New York, and then put on a 17-second loop to be broadcast to New Yorkers on Christmas Eve. I have a yellowing typed copy of the original *Yule Log* memo that he circulated to the station management staff. It's dated November 2, 1966. It reads:

> On Christmas Eve, Saturday, December 24, there is a hole in the COLLEGE BASKETBALL schedule (which is now firm for this time period starting December 3) from 10 to 11:30 P.M.—which gives us an opportunity to do something a little different and special.
>
> I have a suggestion: That we announce and promote the fact that we are canceling all programs and commercials from 10 P.M. to 12:30 Midnight (we can easily knock out Roller Derby 11:30 to 12:30 Midnight) in order to present a WPIX CHRISTMAS CARD to our viewers.
>
> Our "card" would consist of a piece of color film or tape (which we would have to have made) of approximately five minutes' duration which would be repeated (via a looping process) over and over continuously for two and a half hours. The color picture would open on a beautiful fireplace with Christmas stockings and flaming yule logs and the camera would dolly in eyeball to

eyeball with the fire so that the effect is that the television set be-
came a fireplace.

Audio-wise, we would feature two and a half hours of Christ-
mas music and carols prepared by WPIX-FM (which would be a
great advertisement for them). The radio station could carry the
same program simultaneously and make announcements directing
people to turn on their television sets and bring the warmth of the
yule logs into their homes.

You really have to see this to believe it. The television set ac-
tually becomes a fireplace and since Christmas Eve is a time for
decorating the tree after the children have gone to bed the over-
all presentation should be most effective. And since we would be
canceling all programs and commercials, it is startling enough to
gain attention.

Unless there is something radically wrong with this idea
which I haven't thought of, I would like the station to lay it on—
so, Hank, will you please discuss this "plot" with Messrs Freeman,
Pope, Cooper, Tuoti, and Christian, find out what is involved and
tell me whether it can and will be done.

Fred M. Thrower

PS: The stereo aspect of the sound would not have meaning for TV
set owners but those with both TV and FM sets could turn on their
FM sets for stereo and TV sets for picture.

Viewers tuned into this annual viewing treat for 23 consecutive
years. Even those households with fireplaces liked watching. Several
years after Dad retired, however, *The Yule Log* went off the air only to
return in 2001 due to popular demand. And guess what? The holiday
video—now a four-hour loop with the original collection of Christmas
carols completely remastered—won its time period in New York's local
Nielsen ratings each year since its fiery comeback. Because WPIX is
owned by Tribune Broadcasting, *The Yule Log* went national in 2004

and reached 65 million homes via Chicago-based Superstation WGN. *San Francisco Chronicle* television critic Tim Goodman wrote in a December 2004 column that *The Yule Log* stands as one of television's two or three best ideas, ever!

✓ **LESSON: Coming up with *The Yule Log* didn't involve anything fancy. Dad believed in easy-to-understand communication. But before WPIX could roll out its faux fireplace, Dad first had to convince management of his burning idea. His memo was the spark. These days, a good idea can easily get lost in the corporate decision-making process, a result of petty turf wars or reluctance to try something new. Too often, effective ideas get rejected because they have to travel too far in an organization filled with fiefdoms and inevitable roadblocks. What is required to catch the attention of colleagues or clients is the ability to communicate clearly, concisely, and to the point. A little bit of simplicity and a whole lot of creativity can cut right through those attention-deficit barriers. Nearly forty years after Dad typed up that memo, his fire is still burning bright every holiday season.**

Cutting-Edge Technologies that Will Save You Time and Attention

IT'S AMAZING TO think that when you ask people for a phone number, they almost always look to their mobile phone, and they seldom remember it. Why? Because people don't rely on full phone numbers anymore; they have a speed-dial location in a mobile phone, or a place in their computer database. The challenge then is to really learn about all the time-saving and attention-grabbing techniques that are out there. For example, did you know that you can send text messages from web browsers to someone's phone or that if you want to send a text message to any Verizon customer, you can simply type their phone number@vtext.com as an e-mail and it will automatically be sent to their phone? Twenty years ago, it was, at first, very impressive to send someone a fax. Then it was necessary to page someone, then voice mail, and now it's the mobile phone and the text message.

Stay on top of the technology of time management. Another example is the Voice-to-Web technologies that some carriers offer where your voice mails are sent to you by e-mail. Additional time-saving and attention-grabbing technologies include the use of digital photos embedded in e-mail. Learn how to use HTML software to program response mechanisms or multiple choice e-mails that create a simplified response. I remember sending a 10-question electronic questionnaire to student travel whiz Mike Fuller, who purchased my first company, The College Connection, in 1997. Mike, because of his busy schedule, was notoriously difficult to contact. Labeling it an "answer quiz," I e-mailed him all the pertinent information in a 10-question quiz, which required "yes" or "no" answers or multiple-choice answers. He found this entertaining and the response came back to me within twenty-four hours.

✓ **LESSON:** Seek out and capitalize on as many time-saving technology advances and techniques as you can. Identify the things in your life that slow you down. Review and modify the list of people in your cell phone's speed dial every month, because your priorities change, and the people you're working with change. Read the instruction manual for your mobile phone and e-mail program. Continually adapt your focus and develop a technology toolset to help, not hinder you.

Weapons of Mass Distraction: Hidden Agendas

WHAT IS THE hidden agenda? Put simply, it's a non-disclosed goal, or a secret plan of attack that someone is keeping confidential. We should acknowledge that in business, due process may actually mean "anything you say can and will be held against you in a management meeting or job review." However, with hidden agendas, it's often what you don't say that can hurt you.

The dreaded hidden agenda can spread through organizations like a disease. It can come down from the top, or it can start somewhere in the middle. But once it's unleashed inside a company, it's hard to remove.

There are several techniques to uncover someone's hidden agenda. Be honest and just ask them, "Now what are you trying to achieve here?" You can also put yourself in their shoes and try to determine why they are not telling you something. You might be able to decode some of their intentions this way. By taking a particular interaction and breaking it down into a "value exchange," (in utilitarian terms, this means who is getting what from whom), you can bring to the surface elements of the agenda that remain hidden. If you want to get scientific about this, make a detailed list of the valuable and unmentioned things one party can get from another party, and vice versa. Usually this value exchange will expose the hidden agenda.

How to cut through the red tape of a hidden agenda? Just ask. Break the ice. One way to get someone to open up is to say, "Hey, I'm a very open person, and I can't stand dealing with hidden agendas, so can you tell me, clearly, honestly, and concisely what it is you would like to achieve?" Often this is where the other party begins to squirm, and this is where you need to be a relentless investigator. Continue asking follow-up questions. Sometimes it helps if you reveal your agenda first.

It is not always easy to simply ask someone what his hidden agenda is. History repeats itself, because people don't often change; they just become more entrenched in their ways. So study their past interactions, business deals, and contracts.

I remember one group who met with me at Active. They came to the conference room, set up, and then went to the rest room because they had been in traffic on the drive from Los Angeles. When they returned, they noticed they had left their binders open to an internal list of their formerly hidden agendas with our company—one of which was to get us to invest or buy them because they were out of money. Without our financial help, they would be out of business in three months. With this knowledge, we had the upper hand. It would have been more productive for both sides if we had found out that the company was in trouble from them. We would have been able to trust them—and a deal might have been possible.

✓ **LESSON:** It may be apparent when someone has a hidden agenda with you or within your organization. At other times, the agenda can lurk undetected below the surface of an interaction like a hungry crocodile. Some people are so skilled at hiding their agendas that their behavior is almost pathological.

Sometimes hidden agendas are necessary, but most often they are a complete waste of everyone's time. They consume energy and resources. They are an unwanted distraction. In today's fast-moving business environment, the basic rule is this: Uncover hidden agendas immediately. Tell people what you are trying to achieve with them, then ask them what they are trying to achieve with you or your company. Take the time to list what you think people could want from you, and list the things you want from every interaction. Always know what you want, and find out what they want. Strip the agendas of their protective armor. Naked, not veiled, agendas will turbo-boost your productivity and efficiency.

Star in Your Own Reality Television Show

APPEARING ON A reality television show is not as glamorous as it sounds; in fact, it can be tiring. When I was approached by eight-time Hawaii Ironman World Champion Paula Newby-Fraser and asked to be on a sports reality show with several other triathletes, I jumped at the chance. A few weeks later I found myself living with a camera crew and a producer. They were great folks, all from the Fine Living Network, and they were filming a show called *Fantasy Camp*, covering four people taking part in a triathlon training camp in Kailua-Kona, Hawaii. We filmed some great activity, including a spoof version of MTV's *Cribs* to some meaningful interviews and training on the lava fields.

To me, the biggest surprise was that we shot probably 40 hours of video that would eventually be condensed to a single 26-minute show. When you're filmed, you can remember the scenes. But when you see the final product, you realize how much was edited out. The final version was a compressed snapshot of a five-day period.

In a conversation with high-powered Hollywood dealmaker Conrad Riggs, who works closely with Mark Burnett, the reigning U.S. emperor of reality television with prime-time hits such as *Survivor* and *The Apprentice*, he said, "Mitch, reality shows work because they offer an unscripted portrayal of life, and the reality is that life does not have a script."

✓ **LESSON: In any attention-deficit environment, we witness experiences condensed into sound bites. Like our memories, we remember some of our experiences, but we certainly can't remember every detail. Try thinking of your memory as a digital videotape. Imagine that that tape has been running in your mind since birth.**

But your playback can only access certain experiences and activity. Where is the rest? Buried where? Deep in the unconscious? Forgotten? What I realized after working in front of the camera for a week in Hawaii was that we are all stars of our own reality TV shows. We are the participants, producers, editors, and viewers. What others remember about our behavior is often edited. And what we remember about ourselves and others is similarly self-edited.

The Bunker-Busters:
Come Out with Your Money!

IT WAS A cold wintry night in Washington, D.C., in 1944 when Dad heard a static-filled radio presentation featuring Joan Fontaine passionately reading the "White Cliffs of Dover," with the orchestra playing in the background. Her words reverberated, "Never have I loved England so dearly and so deeply . . ." Having been moved by the emotional tides of World War II, the next morning he resigned as vice president of sales for NBC in New York City and joined the Navy. During the war, he landed in Normandy and then led a special Media Unit on the front lines. He was charged with talking the Germans into coming out of their bunkers and forts and surrendering.

Perhaps this is where I learned how to raise money in an investment climate that resembled WWII bunkers. When Dad would approach the Germans in a specially modified jeep carrying amplifiers and directional speakers, he would tell his translator to convince them the war was over—that the Allies were winning. He had one primary directive: to always tell the truth. This is not unlike my discussions with venture capitalists and investors when they were in their own bunkers during different phases of the tech sector boom and bust.

When Racegate raised its first $5 million from Southern California's largest venture capital firm, Enterprise Partners, we had already received a rejection letter from someone at their firm. I wish I still had that letter. It was the classic "We've reviewed your business and are not interested in pursuing an investment with your company, but we wish you the best" kind of letter.

Several weeks after receiving this rejection letter, my team participated in the University of California's San Diego's Connect program, designed to improve our business pitch. The panel included a lawyer, a banker, and a venture capitalist. That sounds like the setup to a joke: "A lawyer, a venture capitalist, and a banker walk into a bar . . ." The venture capitalist was Ron Taylor, who had been a visionary and a successful entrepreneur. After the presentation, Ron provided recommendations for our company. Ron's thoughts were bright and very helpful. Following the meeting, I invited Ron to tour our offices. He was inspired by what we were working on and he engaged in a lengthy process of helping our venture, even though his firm had already turned down the investment.

A few weeks later, Ron produced a term sheet and Racegate became the first participatory sports software company to raise institutional capital. What is critical to realize is that when you are requesting money from someone, you don't want to say, "Hey, come out of the bunker so you can invest in my business." Instead, ask for their thoughts on how to make your business successful.

✓ **LESSON:** Asking for help, rather than money, is the true bunkerbuster in venture capital. And, like my dad did with the Germans in WWII, tell them the truth. You must acknowledge when investors don't want to climb out of their bunkers. To get them out, sometimes you have to send messages that are loud in content, not in volume. Approach the people who influence them. Get someone who speaks their language on your team. The easiest way to get a VC out of his bunker is to ask for help on a project, not ask for money. If I ever find the original rejection letter from Enterprise Partners, I will frame it next to the received wire pledging a $5 million investment.

You've Got S-Mail!

FIRST THERE WAS mail, then there was e-mail. Now we have "s-mail" which is the ultimate time-saver. *It's not snail mail. It is subject e-mail.* We already have enough e-mail—wanted and unwanted—clogging our attention arteries. S-mail is nothing more than putting your entire e-mail message in the thin subject field. Space is at a premium here, so your message better be brief. Plus, what is visible in the in-box contains even less space.

After clicking "Read," you just read the subject line or take direct action with the relevant part of the e-mail message. If the e-mail window below is blank, then s-mail is almost like text messaging with your computer. With the proliferation and interaction between computers and remote executives on BlackBerries or handheld devices, s-mail is direct, fast, and to the point.

I've been using s-mail for more than a year now, and I was impressed to see that my friend Keith Simmons, who is the president of XTERRA Wetsuits of Virginia, requires his staff to start off the subject line of each e-mail sent within the company with any of the following: ACTION, NO ACTION, READ, or SEND TO. This way, decisions embedded in the e-mail are communicated much more effectively.

In fact, in writing this book I have used s-mail with my longtime friend and editor, Bill Katovsky, who coined the term. He had started s-mailing me at the outset of the book's project because he knew how to crack my own attention-deficit barrier. He knew that on occasion I might save my regular e-mail only to read it at some future date, so he wisely short-circuited procrastination by grabbing my eyeballs right away. Guess what? I had to respond. Quick and easy.

Maybe in the future, we will have "r-mail." This stands for *reject e-mail.* It would send the e-mail back to the person who sent it to you and communicate that it was not delivered, accepted, or read.

✓ **LESSON:** Use the subject field as your instruction manual for e-mails you send to others in your business or in your life. When you want to direct someone's attention to something important, you have to point. Using the subject line also makes it easier to find and sort your historical e-mails by topic or category. Whenever you send or reply to an e-mail, always change or update the subject line. And make sure it points the recipient in the correct direction. S-mail will save you time.

Learning the Dance of Avoiding Capture in Conflict

DURING ACADEMIC SEMESTERS, I lecture every Wednesday at the University of San Diego as the Entrepreneur in Residence. Since I don't actually have a physical office at the university, I keep office hours in a campus coffee shop called Aromas Café. I like working there because it's less formal. Music's playing. The espresso machines are steaming. It's filled with students studying, talking, and laughing. The place is pure stimulation.

One late afternoon in Aromas Café, I found myself listening to two Brazilians and one American propose to become the central Internet and service provider for the rapidly expanding Brazilian form of martial arts called Capoeira. Capoeira (ka-po-ay-ra) is a very expressive martial art that was developed in Brazil by African slaves more than 400 years ago. It's now popular with celebrities such as supermodel Gisele Bundchen. Slaves used Capoeira to avoid capture in Africa and brought the art to Brazil. It's part dance, part martial arts, where the two participants dance and fight around each other, as if connected by an invisible force field.

What I liked about this team was not only that that they had a very good idea—to be the Capoeira Online Headquarters—but they wanted to bring together a diverse group of passionate people also interested in this ancient dance ritual. This trio displayed genuine camaraderie and I could tell that they had spent a lot of time together. They listened when someone in the group was talking and did not interrupt. They were constantly supporting each other with non-verbal cues and verbal communication. I really liked this team.

I thought back to the many meetings I've participated in. I realized that the dance between companies and venture capitalists often resemble slaves trying to avoid capture, just as in Capoeira. And second, when the executive team doesn't get along, VCs don't want to dance with them at all in a financial relationship. I clearly remember when the conflict between the CFO and CEO was apparent during the presentation. I watched the venture capitalist blink slowly when he realized the presenters had issues. He then looked over at his assistant, and raised his eyebrows to express, I'm sure, the following thought: "If these guys can't agree with each other, how will they get anything done?" Ultimately, both the CEO and the CFO left the organization and matters became more peaceful and productive during our ensuing presentations.

Have you ever experienced or witnessed the negative energy of two people in the midst of a conflict? It's a rough road. Interestingly, I've noticed when working internationally that Europeans tend to have a different reaction to arguing. For example, someone in my Paris office was well known for emotional, intense fighting with his girlfriend. They said the harshest things to each other, sometimes in front of the entire office. They said cruel things that would send Americans straight to divorce attorneys. Then, suddenly, after all the harsh words and nasty allegations, they would fall back into one another's arms. It was a roller-coaster of love and hate, but it taught me something about the French. It taught me that momentary expressions of emotion, no matter how harsh, can be forgiven and forgotten, and that after the storm the business can get right back on track.

✓ **LESSON: In this country, displays of extreme emotion in a work environment is not favorably received, yet certain kinds of conflict have an inevitable place in a work environment. We can't expect to agree on every decision. But we shouldn't let our emotions stand in the way of resolving these differences. Getting angry with someone is a wasteful distraction. When a conflict lacks the intention to find resolution, it cuts productivity and ruins lives.**

If there is conflict within an organization, or if you are in conflict with the person with whom you are supposed to present a proposal, you should either clear up the issues prior to the meeting, or

plan to make the presentation alone. In a work environment, conflict shines a negative reflection on you and your pitch. It does not matter who is right or who is wrong. What matters, especially when selling anything, is that people pay attention to, and prefer to work with, people who get along.

When interacting with others, be aware that people are not only paying attention to your words, but also to how you get along with others. If you have the option to present something alone, or with someone you don't get along with, always choose the former. If you find yourself in a conflict, focus on finding a solution rather than plotting a personal attack. Attacking is the lazy way to push someone's buttons. It's much harder to focus on the solution. When conflict appears on your business landscape, learn from Capoeira and don't get captured.

The Delivery Room

YOU CAN ATTEND business school, receive an MBA, and read thick textbooks on advanced management techniques. But you will seldom encounter this critical element of the Attention-Deficit Workplace: setting and delivering expectations.

In the Attention-Deficit Workplace, you must be adept at telling people what you are going to do and then actually do what you say. It's doubly important that you track and communicate what you are doing. Why? Given the high incidence of blame-placing and credit-taking present within corporate culture, you must make sure the organization gives you credit when that credit is due.

Managers have just enough time to check what they are expecting from you. Beyond that, they don't really want to interact. This is also why, when you enter into any situation with a manager, do not simply outline a problem without suggesting two or three solutions. People don't want to hear about problems without solutions.

The real secret to managing expectations? You set other people's expectations. So set them correctly, with breathing room. At the end of meetings when colleagues are expected to take action steps, ask them to repeat their "deliverables," or what is expected of them and when.

I'll never forget one of the most effective phone calls I ever received. It was from Scott Lange, a superb manager and sales executive in New York City. He was working with the New York Marathon on a detailed proposal from Active. At one point in the conversation, he said, "Mitch, just to be sure, have I provided you with everything I said I would? And, more important, everything you were expecting from me?" His words made me realize why he was so successful—he carefully tracked everything he committed to doing.

I also know that when I call or e-mail Active's IT manager, Chad Smith, he will return my call or address the issue within a few hours, if not in a few minutes.

Then there are the flakes. They never deliver on their promises. I was in the process of getting a non-profit company off the ground called Project Active, which was designed to help disadvantaged kids in war-torn countries through sports. I hired a part-time assistant for the project who interviewed extremely well, but then she disappeared. It was actually entertaining. She would tell everyone that she would be at the office, and then never show up. We used to make bets whether she would make it. In two weeks, she came into the office four days. No one heard from her when she left. She still has a binder with some important photos.

✓ **LESSON:** Manage other people's expectations very carefully. If you can't deliver on all your promises, immediately contact the person who has an expectation of you and level with them. Set expectations below what you expect to deliver. In your Attention-Deficit Workplace, tell people what you are going to do, then do it, track it, and then tell people what you did. It really is that simple. In the expectations delivery room, it's your baby.

Do-Over, or the Power of a Repeat Performance

REMEMBER THAT SCHOOLYARD game where if something went wrong, or things got out of hand, someone would yell as loud as they could, "I call a do-over!" Just like that, whatever game you were playing, in the woods or the house, you would start again. In the business world, it's not as easy to stand up at the conference table and yell as loud as you can, "Do-Over!" when things get a little strange. But in 2001, that's exactly what I did.

Having co-founded an Internet participatory sports software registration company, the Active Network in La Jolla, California, was one thing; sustaining its growth with all its financial, management, and employee demands was another matter. By 2001, the tech sector was imploding. Companies were disappearing faster than early afternoon fog. It was suddenly difficult to raise money. So when it came time to downsize, Active was employing close to 250 people in an organization, including quite a few high-level executives who had arrived in cushy style from all the mergers and acquisitions. I saw the writing on the wall. I foresaw a future of time-sapping conflict associated with increased stress caused by downsizing an organization filled with talented individuals. This, to me, as an entrepreneur, was a guarantee of battling egos rather than building a business.

I did not want to be a part of the gathering storm. My relationships with members of the board of directors were strong, and I was the first person to raise my hand and say, "I'll go to Europe for a Do-Over." During the prior year in my job capacity as chief strategist, I had been focusing on planning and expanding into new global markets. I opened up the Canadian markets and worked with a team to secure events and races as part of the Active Network all over the world, including Italy, South America, and Sweden. But when the board decided to halt international expansion until the company achieved positive cash flow, and suggested that I direct my attention to another area of the business, I found myself at a crossroads. And so, in an organization filled with strong-minded, very proficient founders of the different companies we merged with or acquired, I simply said, "Hey, I'd like to take the rights to this business model with me for Europe, the Middle East, and Africa."

As simple as it sounds, I just wanted to learn something new and expand my educational horizons by starting the same business model in new markets. Moreover, it gave me the opportunity to venture on my own again and put together a team to build the organization. I knew that the learning curve would be steep—especially interacting with different cultures and languages from a management and sales perspective.

Before my final decision to leave Active.com, I went on a bike ride in Malibu, California, with a friend and triathlon training partner, Billy Gerber, former president of Warner Bros. and current chairman of the successful Hollywood production company, Gerber Pictures (he produced many films including *The In-Laws* starring Michael Douglas and the remake of *The Dukes of Hazzard* with Jessica Simpson as Daisy Duke). I wanted to hear his perspective about leaving a company. On that ride, Billy said, "Mitch, you're telling me that you have created the opportunity to go abroad and build a company? Get on that plane immediately. You'll be a much more interesting person if you spend a few years building a company in a different country. You're not married yet, and don't have any children, you have to do it now!"

I took Billy's recommendation and started the uphill negotiation to license the technology from Active. I started the process of finding a team of like-minded entrepreneurial partners and investors to build the business from scratch. I decided that my new business headquarters would be on an enchanting tree- and café-lined street known as the Cours Mirabeau in Aix-en-Provence, France. Not far from the French Riviera, this village had the feel of a French La Jolla. I needed a wonderful work environment because my new company could also hand out what are called "lifestyle dollars" to the people who joined the team.

It was tough going with my Do-Over since the global financial landscape had suffered a severe meltdown following 9/11. Fundraising was not fun. But we kept plugging away, and successfully raised $2 million in angel, team, and vendor financing.

Over the two-year period of building the new business, Active Europe successfully launched in seventeen markets, five languages, six currencies, and twenty-seven countries. Coming full circle, in early 2005 we sold Active Europe back to the Active Network. In this buy-back, Active again became a global company.

✓ **LESSON:** Take a risk. Be bold. Too often, people are afraid of losing their prestige inside a company by venturing outside it. People seek solace and comfort in a predictable job environment, even as it's downsizing. Why spend days and sleepless nights waiting for the axe to fall or stressing over a shift to new work responsibilities after the business changes its objectives? Instead, pay close attention to the direction of your company and the direction of your career. They are not always one and the same. If they diverge, why not take your skills and experience and use them to your best advantage? A Do-Over is much better than Game-Over.

Managing Up

AT THE ACTIVE Network 2004 holiday party, we were all asked to raise our hands if we had been with the company for five or more years. Only a few of us proudly raised our hands. We glanced at one another and the feeling I had was a less stressful version of what WWII platoon survivors probably experienced. After years of fighting together, we shared many common experiences, including surviving at one company, which is certainly not the norm in the tech sector where rapid career transitions rule.

Standing next to me at the party was Active's Human Resources Director superwoman, Dianne St. John, who had been with Active for five years. We looked at each other with a certain understanding, having been through three mergers, five acquisitions, and several periods of downsizing and subsequent expansions.

We talked about what we'd been through. "Mitch, I just want to say that I appreciate everything you've done to create this organization," she said, "and I wanted to say thanks for giving me a thumbs-up in the interview five years ago."

I replied, "Dianne, you've done quite a bit of heavy lifting around here, and I can clearly see that. You've hired well over 90 percent of the current team—that is quite an accomplishment."

"Well, there are a great many things that management just does not have time to know, and that always leaves people feeling a little under-appreciated. For example, you know the sub-minute management drill here at Active: Tell me how you have solved or plan to solve something," said Dianne.

"I know what you mean—the only thing that people are concerned with is how you can fix a problem, not the details of the problem. Active's management team is results-oriented. It hires people to solve problems, not to pass them along the decision food chain. When you waste time on the details of a problem, it diminishes the time you can spend fixing it. No one has the time to listen to other people's problems, and few people would like to take on the responsibility of other people's challenges because everyone is so busy.

"And you know," she continued, "even with me, I've got to get whatever I have to say down to just a few minutes, because everyone is so busy in our company, and things are moving so fast."

"Things are moving lightning fast," I replied.

"That's why I try to train our staff to 'manage up,' " she said.

"Manage up?"

"Yes, manage up," she replied, "because our managers are often extremely busy with new major initiatives, therefore our employees need to manage their managers."

Standing there on a balcony in La Jolla, looking at our organization dressed in holiday attire and socializing with each other, I thought, what a great idea! Manage up. It is unfortunately true that employees in manager-employee roles frequently sit back and take a passive role, waiting for direction, waiting for assignments, or waiting for communication. It's a solid organization where initiative and accomplishment-oriented communication happens in both directions.

Managing both ways (up and down) is more like a marriage than a job. By taking an active role in managing your manager, you will suddenly find yourself discussing ways to make your communication and interaction more effective. For example, you might choose to tell your manager the best way to assign you a task. This could be done via e-mail, or in person. You may even find yourself scheduling a time to review his or her performance as a manager (just be sure to do this gently and supportively). Remember to clearly communicate with them and to take the time to understand when and how they want to interact. Don't be afraid to speak up and make recommendations— how you can work together better, or how they can manage you more effectively. For example, if you're motivated by positive encouragement rather than negative reinforcement, tell them. Set up a manager review session with them and let them know what you've discovered and how you'd like to handle it. Obviously, it's important to develop a strong relationship that does not threaten them in this interaction, and the goal of the review should be to make you more effective in accomplishing what is expected of you.

✓ **LESSON:** Don't be shy if you feel the need to manage your manager. Working underneath others often means an ongoing contest to win their attention. Therefore, make sure to learn about their working style, their listening style, and when they like to be approached. Monday mornings, ten minutes after someone walks into the office, is probably not the best time to address what is bothering you. Spend time thinking about how they can work with you more effectively. Is your manager a good listener or does he or she prefer to see everything on paper? Some people are auditory learners and others are visual. If you mention something to a visual learner, he or she might not remember it 24 hours later. If you write it down or send an e-mail, it might stick. Talk openly with your manager about how to have a productive relationship. Help those above you manage you and you'll survive years of shakeouts.

Getting Your Résumé Noticed

I'VE REVIEWED HUNDREDS of résumés in the past ten years, and I remember one that immediately grabbed my attention. It was for a business development position at Active Europe. The résumé listed his previous job experiences, but the last job he had listed on his résumé stunned me. He had listed his employment with my company! And with the same job title of the position I was interviewing him for. What pretension, I thought. What chutzpah! He then went into detail about all the fantastic things he had accomplished for our organization—increasing sales by 200 percent in our marketing group, building a great team, securing a new client that we always wanted. It was an impressive performance. I almost wanted to call him right then and congratulate him. His timeline into the future was brilliant. He listed his start date as the day of the interview. Not only did he get my undivided attention, he later got the job.

When it comes to the hiring process, you want to get the attention you—and your résumé—deserve. Here are some quick pointers:

1. Make sure the paper is unique, and attach something that represents you; for example, a photo of something meaningful, an example of your work, a sample of your correspondence, even a nice copy of a letter of recommendation.

2. Keep the résumé clear and on target for the job you're seeking. For example, don't send a résumé for a sales position with a mission statement that includes plans to build a marketing department.

3. Never send in a blind résumé (a blind résumé is a résumé that lands in the human resources department without a

reference). If you want to work for a company, then map your way through one of the individuals who works for that company. Call the assistant to the CEO or Marketing VP, or get his or her e-mail address. Get them to forward your résumé to human resources. Make this entry as high up in the organization as possible.

4. Read the book *Rites of Passage at $100,000 to $1 Million+: Your Insider's Lifetime Guide to Executive Job-Changing and Faster Career Progress in the 21st Century* by John Lucht. It details several techniques that have been used successfully to obtain many jobs, not just the $100,000-plus jobs.

5. Don't make your prospective employers do their own research about the companies you've worked for. Let them know what those companies do as part of your résumé.

6. Your résumé should be no more than two pages. A résumé is not unlike a movie trailer. You want to nab someone's attention as fast and efficiently as possible.

7. The all-important cover letter should identify your link to the organization. It can also be a link with a person in the company. It should be brief and strong. *Always add a P.S.— most executives read the P.S. first.*

To get your résumé noticed, persistence helps. In 2004, I hired an intern at Active Europe. Leonard Ward rapidly became our star associate intern and we eventually hired him. Leonard made the extra effort. As a student in a business class in which I guest-lectured at the University of San Diego, he approached me after class and handed me his résumé and cover letter. Both let me know that he could be of great value to the organization. I scanned them and put them in the "next month to review" pile. He called me at the office the next day, articulate and bright. I let him know that I was heading out of town and I would introduce him to someone when I got back. He then made it very clear that he enjoyed my lecture, and he wanted to come and learn from me, by working for the company I was in the process of building.

During his visit to my office, when he overheard several phones ringing in the background, and saw that two people were waiting outside to meet with me, he said that he would work for free for two weeks. If, after two weeks we were not convinced that he was essential, then he would return to his search. By his third day at Active Europe, my senior vice president and I were convinced that he would be critical to the company. Every task we assigned, every project he was given, he tore into it and completed it faster than we expected. We piled more work on him. And though he was still a full-time student, he was accomplishing more in his three days with our group building the European side of the business than others were in an entire week. We were impressed, and we offered him a job.

✓ **LESSON:** Spend the time to go the extra distance with your résumé, and in the process of getting your résumé to the right person. The challenge inherent in creating your résumé is to deliver a document that informs your potential employer not only what you have accomplished in the past, but through interpretation, what you can accomplish for them in the future. Think creatively about how to communicate what you can do for an organization. Consider giving a company or an individual two weeks of your time to convince them that you are essential. Be persistent and nudge your way in, or have someone else give a helpful nudge for you.

TGIF—Thank God it's Friday

FOR YEARS, I'VE been riding a psychological wave that has led to financial and business success by utilizing the power of Fridays. We've all heard the saying "Thank God it's Friday," or maybe even dined at the restaurant chain know by the TGIF initials. But when I repeat this phrase, it's for a different reason. I love Fridays simply because around the world, people's mental states undergo a distinct change on the fifth day of the work week, making it the single most effective day to get what you want from business associates. Even the most gloomy, downbeat people can be found smiling on Fridays.

I always schedule my important calls and important meetings on Fridays. I've also consistently made sure that any time I ask someone to write a check, to invest in something, or pay a client bill, it's on a Friday.

I also like to present business development concepts and marketing proposals on Fridays because it provides more time to work on a professional follow-up over the weekend to be delivered early the following week. You will be amazed how much easier it is to get people to say "yes" on Fridays.

Because people naturally decompress on Fridays, you can develop a relationship with people in your business network a great deal faster if you consistently call and interact with them on this day. Just imagine someone who always calls you on Friday, and another person who always calls you on Monday. On which day do you think you'd be more likely to: a) listen, and b) say "yes"?

✓ **LESSON:** Call people of significance on Friday. Ask for payments on Friday. Make your important presentations on Friday. Because of the positive energy built into this day, think of Friday as the day of Yes.

Multitasking

IF YOU HAD happened to watch the 9/11 Congressional Hearings, this expression came up a lot: "I was tasked . . ." It meant that a particular assignment or responsibility has been requested from that individual. In the Attention-Deficit Workplace, however, we aren't just tasked; we are multitasked. And who's often doing the asking? Surprisingly, we task ourselves.

The layers of multitasking can run very deeply in our daily lives, but if you don't understand your own personal multitasking capacity, your efforts will quickly fragment your thoughts and start to impair your work. So how do you effectively do more than one thing at a time?

First, start to understand how you currently multitask. Take a day and monitor yourself. Watch how many times you attempt to do more than one thing at a time. Now make a list of the things you do in tandem, and the things you've left undone. What are you most effective doing at the same time? What knocked you off track on some projects? Was it attempted multitasking? This will allow you to discover your personal capacity to multitask.

There is no question that technology can help you multitask: the wireless headset for your phone, the wireless modem for your computer and remote access to your files and e-mail all free you from your desk or your cubicle. But if you need to focus on a project, make sure to limit your multitasking.

Remember that it is very important to communicate to the people around you when you are multitasking. One recent associate, Katie Tye, a graduate from the University of San Diego, would ask me, "Mitch, how much of *you* do I have right now?" And I would answer, for example, "You've got 50 percent." She would either say, "That's fine, that's all I need to let you know that I need you to take this call." Or she would say, "Let me know when I can have 90 percent of you, because I have an important change to your proposal." Katie and I were engaged in team-enabled multitasking.

These pointers will help you multitask more effectively:

1. Know how many mental programs or physical projects you can run effectively.

2. Identify the programs, people, and projects that require 90–100 percent of your attention.

3. Tell people when you are multitasking, and let them know they can always ask for your full attention.

4. Track your projects and programs so that you can multitask them all to completion, not to a desk full of incomplete items.

✓ **LESSON:** In the movie *The Remains of the Day*, Anthony Hopkins plays an uptight butler and Emma Thompson the head housekeeper in a stuffy English country home. At one point, they are taking a walk together. The younger woman is talking quite a bit, and so he casually mentions to her, "Do you know what I am doing, Miss Kenton? I'm placing my mind elsewhere while you chatter away." He was doing at least one thing right; he was letting her know he was multitasking.

Always let people know when your attention is elsewhere. Spend time to understand your own multitasking capacity, and your projects and goals. List them. Work with people when you multitask; don't simply tune them out. Working on several projects at the same time can add insight and a relief from boredom. If you manage your multitasking, you'll be much more effective than if you simply hop from project to project without driving them to completion. Multitask your way to success, not distress.

"The Smartest Guys Win"

EVERY NOW AND then, I phone my friend Steve Hansen for advice when I'm in the middle of tough negotiations or trying to unravel a complex, thorny financial issue. He's my go-to guy. His instincts, judgment, and experience were battle-tested in the financial services, entertainment, and technology sectors. Trained as a financial guy, he skyrocketed through the ranks of KPMG Peat Marwick to become a partner in their media practice in Hollywood. From there it was on to Universal Studios where he became senior vice president and chief financial officer for a big chunk of Universal Studios. Over his five years at Universal he raised several billion dollars of debt and equity to finance their domestic theme park and hotel expansion in Orlando and led the early stages of the $1.3 billion financing of Universal Studios Japan. He then made a pretty big career left turn and joined GeoCities, an unknown Internet company in Southern California. During his two years with GeoCities as CFO and COO, Steve managed the company's final round of venture financing ($75 million), the company's initial public offering in August 1998 and eventual sale to Yahoo! for $5 billion. After sitting on the beach for a while, Steve recently joined the ranks of a venture capital firm investing in early stage technology companies.

These are a few of the career milestones in my friend's successful business life. In the process of writing this book, I thought it would be instructive to hear his personal take on attention, time, and people management. Here then are some snippets from our hour-long conversation, including what it felt like to be yelled at by 83-year-old Lew Wasserman, the legendary all-powerful founder of Universal Studios.

"At GeoCities, we had grown from being worth $90 million to around $5 billion in 14 months and I mean, the place was going 120 miles an hour, non-stop, every day. As the Chief Operating Officer, I had eight or ten different departments and about 300 people reporting up to me. The only way I was able to get things done was to be able to multitask at a rate that was very different from most of the people around me. Fortunately I had enough discipline and energy to simultaneously manage many different things. That was 1999 and we were living in the nexus of the entire Internet explosion, so the stakes were very high. To the extent you, as a manager, can actually do that successfully and in a way that doesn't kill the people around you—you can actually get a tremendous amount done. But the collateral damage can be significant and ultimately that pace is simply not sustainable."

I asked Steve: "How were you as a person to work for and with?"

"Candidly, I was really difficult. Not mean, but very focused. I think I'm a lot better now. I was curt, overly direct, and totally driven. I didn't have time for the pleasantries that, frankly, human condition and Management 101 says are necessary to keep those around you motivated. For me, the work effort was an almost clinical process, where I really didn't have time for anything other than what was critical to get the job done. I was not a warm fuzzy guy. Steve Covey would have been horrified.

"When I left Universal Studios for GeoCities, I went from being a guy in an Armani suit making $600,000 a year with the big corner office on the studio lot and my own secretary, to an 80-square-foot office in the worst part of Santa Monica, where the elevator smelled like urine and seldom worked.

"And I had taken a $450,000 a year pay cut to go do it. Anyway, the first week or so I was at GeoCities I found myself in a breakfast meeting at Bucks Diner in Silicon Valley with Tim Koogle, or TK, the CEO of Yahoo!. With TK at the breakfast were other top guys from Yahoo!: Jeff Mallett, president, J. J. Healy, senior vice president, and Jerry Yang, co-founder. Anyway, they had all just been on the cover of *Time* or *Newsweek*. I'm thinking to myself, 'Holy smokes. Here I am, fresh off the bus from the entertainment world, sitting in the middle of Silicon Valley with these guys that I had been reading about for the last two or three years.' As we made small talk waiting for one of my board members to arrive, I asked TK, 'What is it about this whole technology world that you like the best?' Well, he looked me right in the eye, getting this really sly grin on his face and he said in a very low voice, 'You know what, Steve? I love technology because the smartest guys are going to win.'

"And you know what? Ultimately I came to realize that he was right. In the technology world, to a large extent, the natural selection process is alive and well. It's almost a polar opposite compared to the entertainment industry where there is just so much vanity, greed, backbiting, and combativeness. The really shocking part is that a large number of enterprises not only tolerate such behavior; it's actually encouraged.

"What worked at Universal Studios in 1992, would simply not work at GeoCities in 1998. Nor would it work at Yahoo!, Google, General Electric, or IBM. Universal Studios was run by Lew Wasserman and Sid Sheinberg, two of the toughest executives in the entertainment industry. They were honest, smart, hard-driving guys who loved what they did. Among the senior executives, the culture at Universal was characterized by a running joke, which said that at Universal you put two executives in a room together to solve a problem and the one that emerges still breathing is the one you promote. Almost every senior executive in that organization lived with that kind of pressure and was very tough. Truthfully, more often that not, nice guys finished last.

"Lew and Sid believed that you'd get the best thinking if you had a competitive environment typified by creative and business tension. They ran the company in that manner. It has changed now, of course, with Seagram and GE ownership, but it was very much the culture in 1997 and ultimately one of the reasons that I left Universal. The environment was so political and combative, I was spending 70 percent of my time dealing with internal politics and 30 percent actually doing my job. It simply wasn't sustainable. I don't think anyone can go to work every day with a knot in his or her stomach, worrying about whether a superior or a peer is going to take your head off."

I asked my friend, "When Lew Wasserman screamed at you, what did the little boy inside Steve Hansen say or do or think?"

"First off, it was memorable. Lew was a very imposing character. What I thought was, 'Okay, this guy is 83 years old, and damn he's smart. He knows this stuff better than me. I should have been more prepared before I came into this meeting.' And I'll tell you what. Next time when I went into a meeting with Lew or Sid, I was better prepared. Even if it meant staying up all night. At Universal, I elevated my game to a level that I never could have achieved had it not been for being in that crucible. Those guys were very smart and very tough, but it's binary, meaning, in that environment, you either succeed or fail. There's no middle of the road. They didn't scream to complain that their lattes didn't have enough foam or complain about a parking spot.

"Nope, Lew would scream because film sales at the Kodak kiosk in the front of Universal Studios Hollywood, last Tuesday, had been $300 less than they were a year ago and he wanted to know why. As the CEO of a major movie studio, he always knew what he was talking about, down to the smallest detail. He had done his homework. He insisted on the same level of dedication and attention to detail from his executives that he demanded of himself. He used the screaming, coupled with facts and logic to get my attention and remind me that the head guy was on top of things and I was not. And you know what? He was just about always right.

"In my jobs subsequent to Universal I have had to unlearn a lot of those behaviors in order to be successful. I mean, I still have those business combat skills and can trot them out if needed. But by and large, I think an executive gets a lot more done by finding different ways to work with people, because everyone is different and motivated by different things. Plus, if you look at the organization as a being, I think there is a very strong parallel between that and an A.D.D. individual. There are all these cycles simultaneously going on—sales, marketing, finance, human resources, and legal—that require focus, attention, and execution. At the end of the day, they're all competing for the most scarce resource the organization has—which is people's time."

✓ **LESSON:** Every organization brands its particular culture and identity with its own distinctive stamp. The work environment can be super aggressive or touchy-feely; it can be survival of the fittest or warm and fuzzy. But not all personalities thrive in the same manner under the same working conditions. The best of all possible worlds, according to my friend Steve, is to be part of "an organization where you find the smartest people on the face of the planet. And if you can find a way to take advantage of that competitive leverage, you can do extraordinary things."

Winning Food Strategies

I'M NOT A nutritionist, but I'm amazed by parents who think their children have A.D.D., and then feed them sugarcoated cereal for breakfast with sweetened juice. The kids are sent off to school with soda, Twinkies, chips, and a sandwich. It's only natural that these kids will be bouncing off the walls. (And no wonder that childhood obesity is becoming an epidemic in this country.) The fact is, caffeine, sugar, and junk food land kids in schools as well as vice presidents in corporations on attention roller-coasters that impair their performance and cause random peaks and valleys in attention.

One of Active Europe's top vice presidents, Jason Egnal, who started a similar online business in South Africa, demonstrated quite early not only his management skill but also his capacity to eat right in the workplace. Jason would stop at the appropriate time and make himself a healthy meal. The day could be in chaos, and he'd take time out for food. Sometimes it seemed outrageous, but afterwards it always proved to be the right decision. Jason was quite a chef, and from the company kitchens in Aix-en-Provence to La Jolla, he would also always offer to share his healthy fixings with the other employees who would often say, "No, thanks, I had something already." Every day he would consistently make sure to consume the correct nutrition.

I remember when Jason and I met for lunch in New York with one of his associates, who had just arrived from a 20-hour flight. We were both pitching him to invest in Active Europe. As soon as our potential investor took his last bite of his roasted turkey over mashed potatoes and his last gulp of white wine, we noticed he was fading. He was sitting up, eyes closed, snoring, sound asleep—right there at the table. We did everything we could to avoid laughing at the absurdity of the situation. We let him rest for a few minutes. Then, when the waiter came, we ordered a round of double espressos.

The Active Network is a business that's based on fitness and nutrition, so you'd think that the Active Network would be a shining example of a healthy company that watches what it eats. It's not. Though it employs many athletes who pay close attention to their diet, Active still has a vending machine that's filled with candy bars. Venti Starbucks coffee cups litter the office daily.

People have choices, and nutrition is one of those recurring choices we make every day. It adds a cumulative effect to our lives, either around our midsection or around our careers. I've found that the best way to normalize my attention span at work is to drink massive amounts of water during the day, and to eat a healthy breakfast with bread, grains, and fruit. To stay focused, I'll have a sound lunch with a salad, a good source of protein, and small snacks in between like a banana or an apple. For dinner, I try to eat early, with some fish, vegetables, and a light dessert. An important thing is to have very light snacks in-between meals to keep your blood sugar up. When that post-lunch afternoon lull hits, I tend to get up and go for a brisk walk or a jog.

You can study nutrition to learn more specific things about how things like Omega-3 fats improve attention and intelligence. It's not about going on crash diets to slim down. The keys to losing weight and keeping the pounds off are exercise and a proper diet. Your workplace cannot guarantee that you eat the right foods, so it's up to you to make sure that you do.

I have a friend who worked at a now-defunct Internet search-engine start-up in 1996, and he once e-mailed me that the company's management decided that one way to keep its staff of 100 "cyberserfs" motivated was to have a well-stocked kitchen filled with the wrong kind of nutrition. I saved that e-mail because it showed the length to which some companies will go to keep employees tethered to the harmful quick energy of junk food. They were provided with an endless supply of free Calistoga juice, coffee, tea, microwaved buttered popcorn, sugar-glazed bear claws in the mornings, and pizza in the afternoons. My friend said that by late afternoon, he'd be so wired from consuming all that sugar and caffeine that he could barely make sense of what appeared on his computer screen; he was overstimulated to the point of jittery incomprehension. The San Francisco–based company, by the way, devoured more than just junk food; it ate through $10 million in ten months and then went bust.

Now, I've gone astray plenty of times from following a sensible diet and timing plan. So what I try to do is follow the 80/20 rule, which is simple: 80 percent of the time I eat healthy and try to make the right choices, and 20 percent of the time I eat whatever is in front of me. Otherwise, it's too much effort, because paying strict attention to what you eat can drive you batty. When you're on a high-speed train from Paris to London, and you've missed breakfast, it's just silly to try to scrape the mayonnaise from your turkey sandwich while the little kids in front of you are staring at you.

✓ **LESSON:** Proper nutrition is key in avoiding erratic spikes in blood-sugar levels. You want a balanced diet for health and fitness reasons, and to stay focused throughout the day. Relying on caffeine—coffee, colas, and tea—makes your body dependent on this stimulant. (A 64-oz bottle of Mountain Dew has 294 milligrams of caffeine, a 12-oz cup of coffee clocks in at 200 mg, and that 8-oz cup of brewed tea has 50 mg.) Try different foods at different times. Limit your carbohydrate intake at lunch if it makes you drowsy in the late afternoon. Remember, every 24 hours you have to put a whole new block of food into your belly. Unlike your genetics, you do have a choice over what foods you eat and their subsequent impact on your well-being. Your choices will impact your capacity to operate in an attention-deficit environment.

The Art of Negotiation Doesn't Have to be the Art of War

IN 1999, A friend of a friend of a friend forwarded me a business plan from Racegate's largest competitor that had been making the rounds in the investment community. I impulsively decided to pick up the phone and call the firm's founder. This was not something new for me. I had already done the same thing with several other smaller competitors—Get Set Go, Enter Online, and Do It Sports. Early on, I had decided to build Racegate through partnership, organically, and to catapult market-share through acquisitions. And so Racegate grew in size, revenue, and staff by this three-pronged approach. My philosophy was to reach out to the competition instead of fighting them. I downed a cup of Starbucks coffee and with a deep breath, I looked out at La Jolla cove from my office window and dialed Jim Woodman's number in Florida.

"Jim, this is Mitch Thrower from Racegate. How are you?"

"Fine," he replied, curtly.

"I just wanted to say that I've been impressed with what you've accomplished at Active USA," I said, stroking his ego.

"Thanks," he replied. I could tell he liked the compliment.

"I've been following your progress, and I'd like to open the discussion with your group about a merger or an acquisition."

"That sounds interesting. How much?"

"I'm not sure what we'd be willing to pay; we would have to learn more about your organization."

"Pay us? I was thinking we would acquire you," he said.

"I was thinking we would acquire you," I replied. We both laughed and the tension dissipated.

After I got off the phone with Jim, I forwarded him our business plan. I had already received a fax copy of his business plan, so I thought he might as well have ours.

For the next month, we had a series of conversations that eventually ended with a 50/50 merger of our companies—creating the participatory sports powerhouse, The Active Network, and attracting millions of additional dollars in venture capital.

Jim Woodman is one of three original co-founders who has not only survived, but thrived through the chaos of Active's growth. As one of the most determined, focused, and intuitive people I've ever met, Jim's work in all areas of the business continues to drive Active forward.

As Active expanded into Europe and then later, when I started Active Europe, I used the same strategy with an online athlete registration firm based in South Africa. It was the old, "Let's be partners or I'm going to put you out of business" strategy. After several months and a visit to Johannesburg, Active Europe had acquired the leading registration provider in South Africa.

Through two acquisitions I had initiated prior to Racegate's merger with Active USA, I discovered that the most effective way to court my competitors was to be very open right from the beginning, to let them know *almost* everything about my company. At first, one must be open, but not too open until a certain comfort level is reached. It's like a courtship that requires a mutual escalation of trust and respect.

Entrepreneurs and management often spend years huddled in their chilly isolated caves, creating market competition drawings on white marker boards hung on the damp rocky walls. They build fires and fight over what to do in an effort to figure out the competitive advantage over another company. It's a tooth-and-nail struggle for survival and conquest.

Companies spend millions of dollars in cash and millions of hours of human capital battling one another, rather than simply focusing on and delivering the best possible product. Rather than engage in an endless battle, they forget that it's just as easy, if not easier, to pick up the phone and call your competition and say, "Let's join forces."

Sometimes we see mergers on a mammoth scale uniting former foes, such as Hewlett-Packard and Compaq. Each had separate reasons for wanting to merge, but what finally brought them together was a four-letter word: Dell. All of Wall Street takes notice when the giants do their courtship dance.

This dance can start off quite unsteadily. It was rocky when I had approached Tom Silensky from Do It Sports, a Michigan-based online registration company, which had grown steadily despite its small size by servicing some of the major customers in the marathon community. Do It Sports was one of the first companies to offer online registration in the pre-Internet boom days of 1994. For several years, I had called Tom and once even flew to icy Michigan in February to have lunch with him.

Tom and I got along reasonably well. And we shared information freely. In my open-book fashion, I tried to convince Tom to sell his business to Active and unify our efforts to win the global market together.

In a somewhat tense reply, Tom once said to me, "Mitch, I'd rather have my business plucked apart slowly by vultures than concede that I lost the war to you." To diffuse the iciness here, we both laughed.

I flew back to a much warmer San Diego, then to Paris, but Active kept the pressure on Tom. As market conditions changed, our position strengthened since we began to sign away more and more of Tom's clients. In 2004, Tom finally sold us his company and joined our team.

There is a common belief that business is war, but for those who have studied *The Art of War*, by Lao Tzu, realize that "enemies help each other if they are together on a boat that is in trouble." Sharing ideas connects people in a functional, cohesive way.

I've always said, "Court your competition." It's paid off for Active, a global leader in event registration. It now often processes over 300,000 registrations per month.

✓ **LESSON:** Competitive companies are like balls of mercury rolling around on the ground after you break an old glass thermometer; they look like solid metal balls, rolling around as if they would bounce off of each other. But just get them close to each other and they will gravitate to each other and merge seamlessly. People waste an enormous amount of time and energy trying to figure out what the competition is doing, and then strategizing and responding to it. My recommendation? Just pick up the phone and give the competition a call.

The foundation of all human relations is common experience. You have something in common with a competitor, so it should be easy to build a common bond. Grab the phone; get out of the cave. As Lao Tzu says, "Having a conflict is bad. Having a long conflict is always a disaster, even if you are victorious in the end."

Deadlines—Greet and Meet Them

MY INITIAL INVOLVEMENT with *Triathlete* magazine gave me a crash course in meeting monthly deadlines. Magazines must arrive on newsstands and be mailed to subscribers on time, every month. Delays are unacceptable to subscribers and advertisers. The clock is always ticking in publishing. Or you perish.

I had little experience in publishing when I was convinced in 1997 by Bill Katovsky, who was the founder of *Tri-Athlete* magazine—whose title became *Triathlete* after he sold it in 1986 and merged with its competitor, *Triathlon*—to orchestrate a leveraged buyout of the magazine. We had met at a triathlon training camp when he was serving a second stint as editor-in-chief of *Triathlete*. Along with a La Jolla-based business partner, I scraped together the necessary capital and invested in the publication. I now found myself president and chief operating officer in an organization that needed a complete overhaul in sales staff and management. We needed a stern taskmaster to set the operations forward in the right direction. A real deadline disciplinarian. You know, like the drill sergeant in the movie *Full Metal Jacket*.

I was fortunate to find the right man for the job. His name is John Duke, and he ran the triathlon camp in Solana Beach, California, where I met Bill, who had made a compelling case to hire this fast-talking former auto lobbyist who was now a triathlon junkie. Originally, John started out as the magazine's advertising sales director, but within 12 months he proved his mettle and was named publisher.

John is a man obsessed by the clock. Impatient, brusque, rude, funny, and always to the point, he doesn't like to dawdle. It didn't take me, or anyone else in the office, very long to learn never to waste his time. Beware of anyone or anything that gets between him and his work. I've seen him in action. John crushes daily distractions like

Godzilla trampling cars. No wasted minutes in the day for this super-workaholic. I once phoned and asked him to describe his personal view of time management. In his usual gruff why-are-you-bothering-me-with-this-ridiculous-question-when-I-have-advertising-contracts-to-close voice, he nonetheless proceeded to explain his philosophy:

"Time is the framework of my life because I have so much going on. I have basically three different businesses: I'm the publisher of *Triathlete*; a sports marketing consultant for Reebok; and I'm a founder of Multisports.com, a personal coaching and training business. I train about twenty hours a week and surf several times a week as well. I have to fit all that into 24 hours each day and I require at least seven hours sleep so if it wasn't for time management, I couldn't make all that happen.

"I manage the clock by multitasking. I don't let minutes flit by. I don't waste time talking to my friends. I have two computers; I have a headset on my telephone so I can ignore people while I'm talking to them and work some more when they're boring me. I have a silent keyboard, but obviously it wasn't silent enough to trick you. *[I heard him typing.]* I use a BlackBerry handheld so I can stay in touch with e-mail while I'm traveling. I have several cell phones. I'm never out of communication. My time is compressed. Now I have to get off the phone. I have a magazine to run." *Click.* The phone went silent before I had a chance to respond. That's our John at *Triathlete*.

✓ **LESSON: One of the greatest lessons I learned in a year as president and COO, and then in the past seven years as board member and owner of *Triathlete*, is that magazines are extremely productive business units with fixed deadlines. Many times, what is lacking in our work lives is what is so prevalent in magazine publishing—an unmovable deadline. So, create and abide by these "time finishing lines" with your career, your job, even your daily tasks. You don't have to crunch time like Godzilla or John to be successful, but if you capitalize on the power of firm deadlines, you will apply your attention to the necessary and important tasks that are in front of you. Deadlines give you focus. Greet them as such and then make sure you meet them.**

Home Office Alone?

I LIKE STARTING companies out of my apartment. From the early days in Westport, Connecticut, when I rented an apartment/office in a rundown former munitions facility to recent times, when I set up Active Europe from an apartment/office in Aix-en-Provence in southern France, I have come to realize that operating a business from home has its pros and cons. With a home office, it's apparent that the commute is nice, there's cost savings, and you have a built-in home-field advantage. After all, if you commute just two hours a day, that's close to twenty days you can delete from your calendar every year.

But there are pitfalls. Like working late and then waking up late only to open a bedroom door to employees who have been standing there and knocking because they have an urgent issue to discuss.

Running a home office is similar to running a naval vessel. On a ship, people live where they work. The captain can be reached anytime with a knock on his cabin door.

I've seen people set up home offices with families and children running around, in-laws staying as guests. The ever-present list of things to do around the house can seem either more important, or just more fun than say, making sales calls. At home, it's often hard to keep your attention focused on the work task.

Here then are several pointers that can help with effective time and attention management when operating in the home office environment.

1. Make sure to know when to stop working.

2. When you do stop working, figure out a way to put your work away. I learned to keep a closet that stored only work files. And I would make sure to put my work materials away, so

that if I was entertaining guests, I was not glancing over at the proposal on my desk that was half finished—and thinking about it.

3. Build and communicate boundaries. Be very open with the people in your life about what you are working on and the space and time you need to get it accomplished. Do not be afraid to close the door and post a Do Not Disturb sign— make this sign mean something.

4. Get out of the home office often. Find a place where you can be isolated from the home turf, but free to work. Always have a laptop; never be tied to a desktop computer. Take that laptop to a nearby quiet hotel lobby or coffee shop and set up a working environment that you can visit when you need a clear mind and a new perspective.

So when do you make the move away from the home office to a separate workplace? If you are self-employed, you might never have to make the change. But if you are running a small business that keeps growing beyond the confines of your lodgings, my suggestion is to call your local commercial realtor.

In 1999, my two-bedroom, two-and-a-half-bath La Jolla apartment was filled with 35 people all working for the startup Racegate— which later became the Active Network. We were packed in tight. The moment we finally decided to move to a real office occurred after we hired the director of sports programming from America Online. When Mark Appelman arrived for his first day, we had absolutely no space left. People were actually climbing the fire escape and setting up their laptop computers on the rooftop balcony. Others were using the coffee shop downstairs as their conference room. Because we had no office space for him to start working, we actually set up an office for him on the stove in the kitchen. It was time to move.

✓ **LESSON:** Home and work life can blend successfully if you set boundaries and treat the temporal and attention-management balancing act with proper respect. This work-at-home lifestyle can be incredibly satisfying and an effective way to be closer to your family, but if the setup is not managed properly, having a home office can actually distance you from your family, your friends, and even from yourself. Do it right.

Aligning Your Interests

SOMETIMES IT'S OBVIOUS when you first meet certain people that they don't like wasting time—yours and especially their own. When I was initially introduced to San Francisco investor Matt Barger in 2003 by way of an excellent referral from top trademark attorney Tom Onda, I knew within the first five minutes how serious Matt was about business, life, and his athletic passion—triathlon. He's an award-winning age-group triathlete, and one of the most successful financiers in the world.

At our first meeting discussing *Triathlete* magazine, Matt clearly indicated his interest level. Within a few days, Matt sent me one of the most direct, time-saving e-mails I've ever received. For months, I had been pursuing potential investors for this particular transaction, and it was obvious that most of these parties never read the material I sent them. With Matt's short e-mail, it was apparent that he knew the material I sent him almost better than I did. He was more than a quick study. He was concise and insightful. His e-mail stated clearly what his full objective was, where he was from a price discussion, and how we could initiate a partnership. He was fair, clear, and succinct.

Our deal went through with very few hitches. Months later, during an early morning training run in La Jolla before a *Triathlete* board meeting, when I was discussing a complex management issue at the magazine, Matt said, "Mitch, as long as everyone has the same interest, then it's significantly more likely that we will all be successful. Our group invested in *Triathlete* because we think it's a great investment with a great return. The sport is something I am very passionate about, but it's very important to me that the managers all are financially rewarded based on aligned structures with the owners. The way I structure my investments is simple, I try to align my interests with the people who are managing the business, so that we have the same goals."

Matt's clearly stated principle of investing is one of the great rules to follow when you are investing or partnering with someone. Operating in a non-aligned environment leads to hidden agendas and conflict. The companies I've worked with in the past tried to create solutions that worked for management, investors, and employees, but too often in large corporations, the best for everyone is mere lip service to the idea of alignment of interests. Matt's ideal structure for *Triathlete* was pure alignment and motivation.

During previous discussions with other potential investors, my attempts with them were the opposite of Matt's approach. I could tell that they had hidden agendas—lethal trap doors ready to spring open whenever they wanted. People are wrong to think that they can achieve more by not letting people know what they want, clearly and openly.

✓ **LESSON: From compensation planning to goal and budget setting, when the interests of owners and managers are aligned, it significantly decreases the likelihood one will act against the interest of the other. When you are in alignment with the people around you, you are much more likely to travel in the same direction and avoid hidden agendas. When you have different key shareholders with potentially different interests—for example, one would like to sell the business, and another one would like to buy the business—conflict is sure to arise. Avoid the fog and confusion of hidden agendas by aligning your interests.**

The Office Divide: Create vs. Implement

THE WELL-KNOWN DIVIDE between creative people and process-driven people dictates that the people with visionary ideas are devalued by people who implement them, and vice versa. It's a battle between dueling brain lobes: Right Brain vs. Left Brain. To keep this conflict in check, I've learned the hard way that when you have a great idea, sometimes the best way to make it happen within a large corporation is to convince others that it was their idea—to get them emotionally invested in the project.

Still, it is critical to know when you should give away your ideas and when you should hold them close to the vest. If you are firmly in control, give your ideas away freely. If you are not, think long and hard before you give away your ideas to others, and think about how you will document your ideas and recommendations. Sometimes, I laugh out loud when I sit in conference rooms with people who have shared with me their so-called new ideas, which were taken from an e-mail I had sent to them the week before. Other times, I only smile inside, knowing how easily I can come up with another idea.

Stolen ideas can be the stuff of laughter. The scrambling for taking credit in an organization is almost like dogs marking their territory on idea memos scattered all over the room: Lifting their legs, saying, "Mine," then a few minutes later, "That's mine, too."

In 1993, I submitted a science fiction story called *Flare for Life* to a famous talent agency. The story was about a solar flare causing a radio disturbance in time that allowed a son to try to save his father's life before he was killed on the next day. I had submitted it unprotected by copyright (I did not have an agent), and never heard from them. So it was with great shock when eight years later, I received an e-mail from my good friend Todd Adelman, who started The College

Connection with me, saying, "Congrats! I just got back from your movie, and I recognized it entirely from the story you published at Saint Lawrence in 1990." I checked the website for a film called *Frequency* with Dennis Quaid. My jaw dropped and my stomach lurched. Could this be a case of outright theft or an uncanny coincidence? At the time, I thought the similarities between the film and my story were far too great for this to be anything but an act of piracy. I immediately sought legal advice, but after a long chat with a high-powered Los Angeles entertainment lawyer, he counseled me to back off. "If you ever want to write for Hollywood, don't start your career with a lawsuit."

After further reflection, I thought what better way to be acknowledged than having my movie produced, and to not have to have done any work on it! Upon closer look, the story seemed different enough that perhaps someone else really did have the same idea. So I abandoned legal measures. I know that ideas are free, and it would be much easier just to write another, better script. I still cherish the original copy of that story that was first submitted as a class assignment for an English course. Back in 1990, my professor gave me a "B+," scribbling on the front page, "It's too Hollywood."

✓ **LESSON:** If you want others to work diligently on a project, then make it their own. Implementers don't care about the origins of ideas or the creative process; they are too busy with their own concerns, while idea people don't often value the necessary financial and business management skills necessary for execution. Like a Johnny Appleseed, you need to master the art of planting ideas. Start the process of sharing your ideas with someone by asking questions that will lead them to the same conclusion that generated your idea. Make sure to understand the control dynamics within your organization and document the generation of your idea or your movie will wind up getting produced without you getting proper credit.

But as the next chapter suggests, hoarding your ideas should be discouraged in quite different situations and contexts.

Sharing Ideas with Others

TOO OFTEN, WE are stingy with our time and attention needs. Our selfishness and self-absorption makes us blind to others and to the world around us. Generosity needs to come back to the workplace in a big way. I am not talking about year-end bonuses or giving to charity. I am referring to helping others by sharing with them your time and ideas.

I am indeed lucky to have my dad as a role model in sharing ideas. At the end of his life, at age 89, he was suffering from many ailments, including a cardiac condition—a pacemaker and defibrillator were implanted in his chest when he was 79. Even though he was confined to the Intensive Care Unit in New York Hospital, he still bubbled with ways to help others. For example, when he got his hospital toilet kit and saw that the plastic comb had sharp teeth, he dictated a letter to me for the hospital administration that requested the combs not be so sharp for patients. They could accidentally hurt themselves. Another time, when he went under a cardiac scan machine, I brought my Walkman with some Sony professional headphones and was able to whisk him away musically. Sure enough, he recommended that headphones be made available to all patients who were sent into cold, sometimes strange environments. "Music would help the kids not to be so scared," he said.

In the final days of his life, he still wanted to make life better for other hospital patients. This was characteristic of his entire life, especially during his career as general manager at WPIX-TV in New York City. Not only did he create *The Yule Log*, but when Senator Robert Kennedy was assassinated, he did away with all programs and commercials for the day. He just ran one word on the screen: SHAME. Money wasn't everything to my dad. He was always seeking a better way, always something more he could do. He always pushed me to better myself—in every aspect.

We all have the opportunity to change the world around us, one comb at a time. And, at the end, on the fifth floor of New York Hospital, in the cardiac ICU, which is filled with beeps, the smells of medicines, and the sound of ventilators, I finally understood my dad's philosophy as he dictated goodbye letters to his old friends, and where I closely watched how his positive energy to help others was really not criticism, but rather support through recommendations and improvements. Some people help others by wanting them to be their best.

✓ **LESSON:** Being generous with your time and ideas is not an attention drain. You will be surprised at how receptive people can become when you are willing to share with them your expertise, enthusiasm, and energy. Not every idea need come affixed with a price tag. And when others come to you with an unprompted idea or suggestion, stop what you are doing and listen with your eyes, ears, and heart.

Focus, Focus, Focus

AS A SERIAL entrepreneur, I've been guilty of spreading myself too thin when approaching new business projects. To curb this personal attention-draining problem, I first had to recognize that enthusiasm about a new business idea is not the same as pursuing it. I now take a longer view these days. I prioritize. I'm better at weighing costs and risks. I focus my time, energy, and attention.

Seven years ago, I couldn't make the same claim. I had established an investment holding company with a friend. We were simultaneously pursuing overlapping assets in the multisport arena. In addition to investing in *Triathlete* magazine, we started a multisport merchandising company, an athlete travel company, and a wetsuit company. We thought we could leverage off the combined properties, but in reality we were spread too thin and, like butter, we started to melt. Limited resources and the lack of focus forced us to close down several entities and concentrate our energy on the ones that had a fighting chance—namely *Triathlete* magazine, which soon became a lucrative profit center. I learned from this whirlwind period that without focus, nothing you're involved in has a chance.

To borrow a metaphor from baseball, I've become a much keener judge of what to swing at and when to wait. If you ever played Little League baseball, you may have learned not to swing at every pitch. My problem in Little League was that I swung with a smile at everything. When I connected with the ball, my enthusiastic swing knocked it out of the park. But more often, I struck out. In business, you have to stand back and choose your pitch. You'll get job pitches, business development pitches, and investment pitches. You need to be selective.

Once Active.com significantly ramped up with funding and staff, I moved over to business development. My days were spent fielding good ideas from companies who wanted to partner with us. I set up online criteria on our website for new business prospects. Before they could submit a proposal, they had to pass through an online series of hoops and filters, identifying who they were and answering some very basic questions. This screening process saved me time and sharpened my deal-finding focus.

✓ **LESSON:** The right kind of focus is a lot like a laser—a concentrated beam of light. Shine this light only on areas of your business life that make sense. Set up filters to prevent light leaks. What you want to have is the right kind of vision that allows you to swing at the pitch only when it really counts.

Back Up Your Files,
Back Up Your Files

IT HAD BEEN an extra long flight from London, augmented by several hours on the Heathrow runway. When I finally arrived in La Jolla and trudged up the outside stairs with my luggage to my third-floor office apartment on Prospect Street, I felt my backpack opening. Tired or absentmindedly, I had left it unzipped after paying the taxi driver. Now I could feel my backpack suddenly become lighter as its contents spilled down the metal stairs. I turned around and watched in horror as my Sony Vaio laptop started to tumble down the stairs just like a Slinky, and then execute a fearless leap off the balcony, falling two stories and crashing into many pieces on the pavement in front of a sushi bar. The people sitting by the window at Tadashi Sushi witnessed the entire incident.

My heart fell as I walked down the stairs. I had become very attached to this computer. It had everything stored on it. All my business documents, five years of e-mails, all my personal journals, my photos, my video files and even a novel I'd been working on. My laptop was an extension of me. I, too, felt shattered.

I gathered up all the pieces and glumly sat on the curb. I could feel tears well up. In what I thought would be a futile, worthless attempt, I started to put the computer back together. I was surprised to find that the Sony Vaio snapped back together fairly easily. Aside from the screen being fractured and detached from the base and keyboard, everything seemed to fit. I slipped the battery back in place and then I reached down and turned it on. To my surprise, it booted! I looked up to the sushi bar, and people inside were clapping and cheering. It was part Sony commercial, part Hallmark card. I was reunited with the electronic extension of me.

✓ **LESSON:** The most frightening thing about the entire experience was that I had failed to back up that computer for more than six months. Six months of traveling sales meetings, of e-mails, of writing in my journal. All my files were there and they all leaped off my balcony like an Acapulco cliff diver. As soon as I was back at my desk—after carefully carrying my now slightly off-kilter laptop upstairs—I backed up every file. I also vowed to back up files every night, and so I signed up for an online service that backed up my data daily. The one I use now, which is *www.xdrive.com,* offers the security of a daily backup—essential in today's work environment. Sure, you can recover lost data from your hard drive with expensive data recovery firms. But that's not prudent. What about theft or fire? So learn from my laptop's two-story freefall. Make sure your backup is in a different location than the original. It will save you so much time in the future, and it will give you peace of mind when traveling with something as fragile as a laptop.

Repeat Offender

IT'S BEEN MY unlucky fate to often find myself stuck in meetings where the same stories are endlessly repeated. It's as if certain brains had been set on auto-rewind. While repetition over time can improve a story, or embroider it with fictional embellishments, there are two reasons why the same story achieves favorite status for the speaker: 1) It could be because he's found he could make people laugh or pay attention by telling things a certain way; 2) Perhaps he's just lazy.

I once sat in a conference room with two executives in Paris—John was from New York and Vanessa was from France—both of whom I've known for years but who had never met each other before. When they started talking, I sat back. I watched both of them and started taking mental bets with myself to predict what they would say to each other and how they would react to each other's comments. I knew that John would pull up mental CD track #143 about his European vacation and his silly little phrase book because Vanessa was from France. I knew that Vanessa would respond with her mental CD track #42 about getting very sick when she went skiing in Gstaad, Switzerland, because she ate too much cheese in cold weather. I smiled quietly during their inane banter and nodded politely, then excused myself for a phone call.

✓ **LESSON: You know that song you used to love so much? The one you played on repeat over and over again, until it became unbearable? Well, people can do the same thing with their own mental tracks. It is extremely difficult to pay attention to people who are stuck on repeat.**

The quick and easy way to stop people from repeating themselves in any situation, especially in the workplace is to simply say (and don't forget to gently touch that person's arm when you do),

"John, you've told me that story before, and it's an excellent story. I think the point of your story is X, and it's an excellent point." This obviously involves tact and restraint. Remember to always enter conversations with a Repeat Offender with built-in emergency exits, such as saying beforehand that you need to make an important phone call.

The Founder's Dilemma

THERE IS A Gary Larson cartoon with two deer standing up on their hind legs in the forest. One deer has a target on its belly, and the other deer is pointing at it and the caption at the bottom says, "Bummer of a birthmark, Hal." And so it is with founders worldwide. Especially for those founders with less than 51 percent control of the companies they started.

Business schools teach one about the different types of people that are needed in various roles at various times during a company's growth. Corporate cultures almost always require that by-the-book middle managers must fit employees in tidy, neat boxes because they themselves also operate in boxes. The prevailing corporate wisdom can be summed up as follows: "You are responsible for taking care of this part of the business." Everyone is boxed in. Including the guys in shipping who handle real boxes.

Founders are the rebels in this narrowly defined arena, and they don't typically like boxes. They are round pegs in a world of square holes. They move in and out of boxes others devise for them. As visionaries, they are not easily categorized. Founders are, by their very nature, charismatic and can be disruptive. A celebrated example is the Apple tug-of-war between co-founder Steve Jobs and his hired CEO gun, John Sculley. While Jobs eventually returned to Apple and is now its celebrated conquering hero there and at Pixar, his premature exit was messy and ugly.

Personally, it took several early start-up ventures before I realized how long it takes an organization to catch up to my vision for it. A bit wiser and with additional years, I devised several strategies to curtail my creativity and instead focus on driving an organization forward in a linear, methodical fashion. It's one of the reasons I decided to shift my roles and responsibilities at Active during its rapid growth phase.

Strategic planning and expansionary business development may not exist at the top of the organizational flow chart, but it better suited my temperament at the time. I was no longer running a business out of my apartment anyway. We now had investors and shareholders to answer to. So I asked myself, "What part of the business do you like best? Running the office? Or prospecting new business arrangements and finding new partners?" Having entrepreneurial DNA in my blood, the answer was simple. I didn't look at my role change as a lessening of my importance to Active. I was still its co-founder. But I didn't want the company to flounder because my ego got in the way; I actively encouraged the recruiting of a top-tier CEO.

Launching companies can be exciting but also frustrating, because when you can see the future and create companies to prepare the world and people for that future, sometimes you're already operating in that future and your organization is still back in the real world. I've laughed through many run-ins with middle managers and even senior managers that I've recruited into organizations, who have their narrow-minded mapped-out ideas for the future of that organization. Warren Buffett raises the organizational caution flag with what he calls the "institutional imperative," which occurs when a company has so many structural dynamics that it resists change, soaks up the corporate capital available, and has hardwired a knee-jerk reaction supporting bad ideas from CEOs or the board because of what he calls the "lemming-like approach."

The challenge founders face is that they start on the top and they always want to stay on the top, no matter what role they play. I remember a dinner with a CEO. He told me, "Mitch, the problem I have with founders is that you can never get beyond, or promoted, from founder. You're at the top, and it messes with the lines of accountability and control." He was right.

So how can an organization deal with its founders? I say: very carefully. Why? Because if its creator ever leaves the company, he may soon be the firm's largest competitor (although he may have to wait for a few years if he signed a non-compete agreement). So, it's doubly important to analyze both of these angles: one, as a founder; and two, as a company dealing with a founder.

As a founder, you must take into account that you are likely cut from a different mold. Just because your idea is now generating revenue isn't everlasting proof that you will always be right. What matters is what you will receive back from your creation. The rewards from founding a company can be monetary, educational, and intellectual. They can also be spiritual. Your company may also have a social or economic impact in the world.

As a founder, you need to take a step back and understand your place in the value chain. If you want to stay with the company you founded, then figure out a way to work inside the boxes and within the lines.

I remember a meeting in La Jolla when I was presenting the strategic vision for Active's expansion into Europe and the various ways we could expand, but the senior managers and the middle management, with their MBAs and extensive Fortune 500 consulting background, could only see as far as the next quarter. So when I discussed things that were years away, their eyes glazed over. In that meeting, I understood that sometimes a founder's ideas and vision of the future of his company have to be planted carefully inside an organization. People have lives after all; they need to know what they must do tomorrow, and what they should be working on in the next 25 minutes before lunch. I learned that as a founder, it's often prudent to release your creativity only when the organization is in a position to be receptive to your ideas. It's all about timing. Without it, you won't obtain the right attention for your next big idea, even if you're the founder.

As organizations grow from start-ups into larger corporations, there is also new competition for resource allocation between departments. By this time, a growing conflict between founders and the compartmental managers may cause the managers to shut their eyes and ears to the ideas of the founder, because they feel overwhelmed by things existing outside their immediate spheres of influence or to-do lists.

From a company's perspective, founders are unique individuals—the creators—but so too are the managers during different stages of its growth. It takes a special type of person to stand in the room and describe how to create things in the future. And it takes a special type of person who can figure out the daily puzzle of how to make that future unfold profitably.

✓ **LESSON:** Founders may give birth to an organization only to later find a big fat target tattooed on their bellies. Often founders are mismanaged by their own senior managers who might dream someday of breaking out and starting their own company. Founders have to be embraced and empowered within the organization, but their strengths have to be strategically channeled.

The future can be distracting, and companies have to be broken into operational units and departments. A founder might be the first person to push a snowball down a mountain, but a great deal of snow has to be added to that snowball before it becomes an avalanche. A founder should focus on both the monetary and nonmonetary rewards from his creation rather than fixating on the ego that says, "I started all this." The reality is that someone probably came up with the same idea long before the founder ever did, but he happened to be in the right place at the right time.

Password Amnesia

IT HAPPENS ALL the time. We forget our passwords. It's easy to do with telephone banking, online shopping, and web surfing to sites requiring registration (cookies on your computer don't always get recognized, or the host site updates its registration). Some online services require that your password include letters and numbers. Some require at least four digits. Some require more than nine. In the future, some will require that you stop typing and will check via webcam that you first do fifteen push-ups.

There is no uniform format for passwords. In America, you can choose a bank PIN number that is four or five digits, but be aware that if you choose five digits, you will not be able to use that bank card when you are in Europe where the ATM machines are only configured to take up to a four-digit PIN code.

Password Amnesia is that hollow feeling you get when you forget your password to one of the many websites or services you use. This amnesia can strike when you're on the phone with your frequent flyer representative, or when you're trying to buy something on eBay with Pay Pal, both of which require different passwords.

✓ **LESSON: The solution is simple. Start a spreadsheet. Every time you sign up for something, track your password. Remember also to track what e-mail address they have on file, and when you sign up for things, make sure to use your permanent e-mail account. For example, if you have a permanent Gmail account with Google, or a Yahoo e-mail account, then use that one. Track your passwords, and then anytime you need to sign back onto your favorite online dating site or when doing online banking, you can easily access your password file. You might want to name the file** something obscure for safety reasons rather than naming it "Passwords," because that would defeat the purpose of maintaining privacy. Track and pay attention to your passwords and online accounts; it will save you time and allow you to navigate your electronic world more effectively.

Going Legal

ENOUGH OF THOSE stale lawyer jokes. Lawyers have a specific function. They can be valuable assets. You just need to pay attention to the following five rules when dealing with legal eagles. These guidelines apply whether you are working with a storefront lawyer that you found in the yellow pages or a corporate firm on the 40th floor.

1. Lawyers are paid to create issues, but also to protect you from issues.

2. Make sure to have your lawyer invoice you weekly. Not monthly. That way you can keep tabs on your legal bill before it moves into the stratosphere.

3. Pay by the project, not by the hour. That's right. Find a law firm that will take you on as client for a project fee, not an hourly fee.

4. Stay away from large firms unless you have established a special relationship with them.

5. Milk your law firm for all the value it can give you beyond legal services and fees. For example, ask your attorney to introduce you to his firm's other clients' complementary businesses, or whomever might be interested in investing in your business.

✓ **LESSON: Pay very careful attention to your relationship with your lawyer and to the work he or she produces. Pay even closer attention to how they bill you. There is something unsettling about paying very smart people by the hour who like to discover as many** issues as they can find, and then argue about them while the legal meter ticks. Always read all the legal documents that you receive and are in any way related to, or responsible for. Don't trust that the lawyers have taken care of everything. They are not infallible; they often make mistakes. Use your legal team wisely, but remember they work for you.

The Office Romance

IN EARLY 2000, I traveled to Westminster, Colorado, with several members of Active's senior management team. We were there for a tour of the company we recently acquired, LeagueLink.com, servicing Little Leagues and other team sports. Jon Belmonte, one of LeagueLink.com's quirky founders, assembled his staff of 40 in a conference room and introduced us to everyone.

After introductory comments, he then asked the following question, "How many people in this room are currently dating or married to someone else in this room, or in the company?" To our surprise, over half of the staff raised their hands.

Directly after this question, he then asked another: "How many people are related to someone else in this room?" The other half of the room raised their hands. This was a very, very tight-knit company, I thought.

As a self-professed workaholic, I see the basic logic in workplace romance, but I've also seen its downside. Cupid's arrow can strike an emotional bull's-eye or cause a gaping wound. Workplace romances aren't a distraction so long as they bring with them harmony and remain positive. When they turn tumultuous, a lovers' quarrel can affect the morale of entire divisions of companies. This is why people often frown upon workplace romances.

Then there's sex. You can't prohibit sex from consenting partners who are colleagues. (Will we ever see a new hit television series called *Desperate Wives in Business Development*?) Think about it. Being in close proximity with the opposite sex eight hours a day is probably more time than one will spend with one's spouse. There's even a term for female assistants to male bosses; they're called "work wives." This relationship can be entirely platonic, emotionally intimate, affectionate, and is just like a real marriage without the sex, kids, and mortgage.

At Active, I have had the privilege of watching romances bloom between colleagues. In fact, I often joke that we have had more workplace marriages at Active.com than found at eHarmony.com. (The original founder of match.com started his online matchmaking service because he couldn't get a date.) Scott Curry was one of the founders of a company we acquired; he was a genius and critical ingredient to the early success of Active, and began to date a sales manager. They soon became viewed as one, not just to each other but to the entire office. It was as if their identities had merged. When others asked about either one them, it was always, "Have you seen Scott and Kathy?"

Large firms have organization charts and this too often shapes the social hierarchy of a company, and that can unfortunately impact the romantic possibilities within the workplace. In romance, you at least hope that you can operate on an equal basis. But at work, someone is almost always above or below the other person and this can add layers of complexity that a relationship simply does not need. Plus, it can create resentment among the office ranks if say, the $200,000 salaried senior executive is taking long, leisurely lunches with the $40,000 HR assistant.

If you start dating someone in your company, the office rumor mill could chew the relationship up and spit it out before it even gets off the ground. Or it can inhibit or accelerate career advancement for either party. It all depends on how others view your private life, now no longer private. It's difficult to hide a relationship in the workplace anyway. (Should there be a new kind of legal document between consenting partners called the RNDA—the romantic non-disclosure agreement?)

Romance is about building trust, affection, and harmony between two caring people. If romance creates stress, conflict, and distractions in the workplace, then you need to weigh the benefits of love against its cost in impaired productivity. If you are the boss or a senior executive, this trade-off shouldn't be minimized. You don't want to engender hostility and resentment among employees.

I have seen it happen at another company. A co-founder of an advertising agency was dating someone in accounting. He was in his forties, married, and had two young girls. She was in her early thirties and unmarried. They tried to carry on their affair secretly. But after several months it leaked, and when it did, their romance wreaked havoc in the office, leading everyone to take sides. The women were especially bitter. The men were more indifferent. Eventually, she left the firm because the situation became intolerable for everyone, while he stayed on. And now that their romance was fully out in the open, he left his wife and moved into a small apartment. His wife filed for divorce. Several months later, the affair ended. But people at the agency, especially the women, still treated him like poison and didn't want to be around him. The entire affair was more than a time-consuming distraction. It turned co-workers against each other.

Also, what can look like an office romance brewing in the eyes of the hunter can be sexual harassment in the eyes of the prey. Michael Crichton explored this theme in his book, *Disclosure*, which was later made into a movie. Power can be a mighty potent aphrodisiac in a co-ed work environment.

✓ **LESSON:** The workplace may be an optimal place to start a relationship in our attention-deficit corporate environment, but you should be committed to transitioning the romance within several months if it turns really serious. And by transitioning, I mean changing either roles or jobs, or setting very clear work and life boundaries.

A further challenge to workplace romance is the fact that many people end up using work as a cover for an affair. Integrity is one of the essential ingredients to business success, so if you're married and having an affair, you don't want to start the rumor mill spinning or have colleagues start questioning your judgment; you'll no longer be trusted.

If you're starting a small business with your husband or wife, then remember the increased stress from work can easily carry over into your romantic relationship. You need a break from work, and if your significant other is always with you at work, then you need to set up safe zones, or places and times at home where you cannot mention work.

On the bright side, when considering the challenge of dating, where do you want to meet the person of your dreams? On the Stairmaster at the gym, in the cereal aisle at the supermarket, at a night club or perhaps at the stoplight late at night, when looking out the window to the car next to yours, you silently ask yourself, "Could this be the one?" Workplace romances will always have a place in our world; we just have to handle them maturely and with honesty.

Get it in Writing

IN THE MOVIE *Jerry McGuire*, Tom Cruise plays a sports agent loosely based on the life of super agent Leigh Steinberg, and learns that the expression, "my word is stronger than oak," can be more fiction than fact. This wasn't a film solely about "show me the money!" It also exposed a cutthroat business in which greed trumped honesty.

I could relate to Jerry, and there have been times when I've threatened to grab the goldfish on my way out of an office after people agreed to something verbally only to renege on their decision afterward. I've also walked away from business situations when I've discovered that people were trying to rewrite their firm's financial history as well as retool prior verbal agreements in order to make their own personal financial outcome more favorable—at my expense.

The problem with relying only on verbal agreements is that some people forget what they once said, some people don't care what they once said, some people change their mind, and some are cold-hearted utilitarians who always do what is best for themselves no matter how it affects others. Even more surprising, in certain corporate situations, you may find that people too often agree to things that they don't have the authority to implement.

I once found myself in the middle of a heated negotiation with two businesses groups—one team in New York and the other in Southern California—where I learned the lesson about the importance of getting it in writing, painfully, yet again.

In a previous conversation, one of the executives in California agreed verbally that if I were able to secure certain rights for their organization, they would share those rights with the founding team, including myself. These were fantastic, albeit very unreasonable, terms for us to ask for. After nearly a month of negotiations in New York, I convinced them to sign the document with the aggressive requested terms. I booked my flight home to California, and as soon as I got back,

I rushed to the office. However, 24 hours later, I found out that they agreed to accept the special terms for themselves, but they had decided not to grant these terms to the founders, as I was originally told. My heart sank.

✓ **LESSON:** Get it in writing. Recently, the same individual who had agreed to share the rights with the founders in my New York month-long negotiation said to me, about a different matter, "Mitch, I'll agree to that, and I can make it happen." I replied, "With all due respect, I'd rather see an agreement in writing, because you broke the last major commitment you made verbally."

The lines of decision-making are very often blurry, and people forget what they agreed to, or change their minds. It is important to note that this rule holds especially true where the decision-making authority is fragmented among senior management and everyone needs to get everyone else's approval on decisions.

It is also very important to get it RIGHT in writing. Many terms and text can be manipulated by attorneys to confuse you, and to make you agree to things that you or your organization would not otherwise agree to. Your best defense, save marrying a top lawyer, is to keep the agreements simple, and make sure they are done right.

The Ten-Second Rule

KENNETH BLANCHARD WROTE a wonderful business book before the Internet took over our lives. It was called *The One Minute Manager* and it presented core principles that have stood the test of time. It taught us to communicate effectively, to praise someone, to reprimand someone supportively and to set goals—all in a very brief time frame (one minute). This slim title was one of the most concise management books ever written. But if you read *The One Minute Manager* today, you will most likely want to substitute "One Minute" with "Ten Seconds." What once took 60 seconds to achieve is now compressed and compacted into ten seconds. It seems that we are all fast-forwarding our work lives.

Think about it. Ten seconds is about how long the fastest humans in the world run 100 meters. And ten seconds is about how long I listen to many of my voice mails. After ten seconds, if the other party's still talking, I'll hit the *fast-forward* key to get to the course of action, and if there is none, I'll hit *delete*. That's my ten-second rule.

When I wake up in the morning, if I last ten seconds then it actually seems okay to be awake and I can avoid hitting the snooze button on my alarm clock. When I'm at a conference looking for contacts or investors, I know that I've got to hook them in ten seconds. I also know that I need to escape from the vendors trying to sell me a service within the same amount of time, because not everyone follows the ten-second rule.

In our short-attention-span world, ten seconds is not a lot of time. If people only have ten seconds to listen, then you have only ten seconds to get your point across. Of course, you can buy more time if you handle those first ten seconds appropriately. Cold callers know this all too well, and it should take you just about ten seconds to go to *www.donotcall.gov* to sign up for the do-not-cold-call-me list provided courtesy of the U.S. government.

✓ **LESSON:** Ten seconds. That's it. Get to the point in ten seconds. In your ten seconds, you need to outline the desired action or next step. Be clear, simple, and quick.

If you need to make a point, try mentally rehearsing what you are going to say. Otherwise, you might go into overtime and the people you're talking to may tune you out, staring back at you with a blank nod.

You've Been Googled!

GOOGLE IS THE new Big Brother. It has the search-engine goods on just about everyone. Very few of us are spared its sleuth-like ability to reveal details about our lives. If being Googled is an invasion of privacy, well, there's nothing we can do about it.

Newsgroup postings that you might have written in a moment of anger years ago, or if someone posts an image of you, and cites that .jpg file with your name, it will show up on Google.

In 1999, I wanted to see what came up when I typed in Mitch Thrower into Yahoo! search, so I knew what the venture capitalists would see if they were looking online for what I have done in the past.

Mitch Thrower may not be the most common name in the world, but there are several of us out there. The first article that popped up after my name search was a Florida newspaper article that opened "You think it's tough to get a job? Tell that to Mitch Thrower, an out-of-work factory worker who just can't get a job." Then it went on to talk about some Mitch Thrower—in his late 60s in Florida—who just could not get a job. I contacted the paper, the editor, and even the writer, and after three months, it was removed from the Yahoo! search results. No one is under an obligation to remove any articles posted, so convincing the paper, once the article had run its course, was challenging. But ultimately the online editor sympathized with me, and he offered to remove it.

What I recommend doing is that when you know that at some point in your life you are likely to be Googled (also frequently used by those into online dating) is to take the initiative to track the electronic representation of you.

Type your name in. Examine the search results. Then take the time to post the positive things you've done to a website. There are hundreds of services that allow you to post things about yourself online for free, including posting your photos (make sure to name the .jpg files with your name). Create your own private blog. People pay attention to what's in writing about you. You should also remember that they will pay particular attention to what other people say about you, even though it often means nothing. Be aware of what's out there. Search your name in the newsgroups, on the web, and in the images that are posted online. Then take the time to post things that you want the world to see, and what you want the world to know about you.

✓ **LESSON:** Google is free PR. Make it work for you.

Practice the Art of Storytelling

ON A RECENT run through Central Park in New York City with Chris Perera, one of my best friends from college, I asked him for his thoughts on the management within the Attention-Deficit Workplace. A former news reporter for an ABC affiliate, Chris is a highly skilled and experienced television producer. His successes include *The Bravest*, which profiled firefighters pre- and post-9/11, *Body Work*, a reality show about plastic surgeons in Beverly Hills, and documentaries for the Discovery Network.

When he's at his editing bay in his office, he selects the images and the scenes that are designed to demand the attention of viewers. In our post-MTV world, his visual style of presentation is quite different than the days when my father ran WPIX in New York. But there is one element that hasn't changed and, as Chris explained to me, "It's storytelling."

"Storytelling?" I asked

"You've got to tell a story. Everyone loves a good story. Everyone hates a boring story. You should arc the story, which means, when telling people, don't give away the punch line in the first moments, lead up to it, then hit them with it. That's a wrap. Every interchange with anyone you talk to has a punch line, but in business it's called the point. In production I call it the 'Punch Point.' When you're working with people or filming for people, make sure whatever your point is, that it's framed and positioned correctly. Otherwise it will get tangled up in whatever experiences they've already had with your point."

We started running up a hill, so we both paused for a few minutes.

"Know what, hands down, is peoples' favorite topic?"

"Themselves," I replied.

"Exactly," he said. "And the twist is, the best way to get some-one's attention is to pay attention to them. You have to ask them questions about whatever interests them. To build instant rapport with people, you've got to ask and listen. People pay more attention to you when you're listening to them. Attention is a funny thing. People love to talk about themselves. When I try to get someone to sign a release and be on film or to pay attention to one of my projects, the first step is to pay attention to them, to find what interests them. I'm in the business of attention. TV and film make money because people pay attention to the shows, to the ads, to the ideas."

✓ **LESSON: Our daily lives have built-in narrative arcs. A beginning, middle, and end. When relating a story at work, think of ways to make what you have to say interesting and compelling. By the same token, listen carefully when another person has a story to tell.**

Pay Attention to Yourself: Top Ten Personal-Needs Checklist

I'VE SEEN COUNTLESS executives—in New York, San Diego, London, Paris, and San Francisco—burn themselves out through stress and the demands of the Attention-Deficit Workplace. I've even sat bedside with executives who have had near-death experiences from physical complications enhanced by stress.

In today's fast-paced work environment, many around you will try to consume your time and attention, while making sure you know they do not have any time for you.

So to protect yourself from the hazards of the Attention-Deficit Workplace, you also need to pay attention to your own needs. It's a wise investment. It's often time alone that is lacking in our attention-starved economy and personal lives. Chances are you'll be a much less resentful, and much less stressed-out person if you've made the commitment to make the time for yourself in the workplace and in your home life. Here's a quick Top Ten Personal Needs checklist:

1. Learn what interests you in a work environment.

2. Identify the things that distract you from your goals; contain or eliminate them.

3. Pause often. One of the best things you can do when the world is storming around you is to pause. Look around. Then jump in to a project or a conversation at the right time.

4. Get physical. Sedentary jobs allow mold to form on your attention span. Find your way to physical activity, which will clear your mind and help you prioritize the rest of your life.

5. Break impossible goals into smaller achievable steps that you or your team can accomplish. Big, bold goals are almost always achieved in bite-sized chunks.

6. Food is fuel. Eat right. You'll function better and you'll think more clearly.

7. Pay attention to your high-energy personal daily clock. If there is a period of the day when you are most effective, then use this period for your most important tasks. Find out the same about the people you work with, and engage them during their peak hours.

8. If you encounter someone who procrastinates, reward them when they achieve something or turn in a project. If it's you, do the same.

9. Communicate clearly the first time, and avoid any extra verbal expenditures. Stay on topic.

10. Take inventory of your capacities and those of your workplace; direct those capacities towards achievement.

✓ **LESSON: Take care of your own needs. You can't always change the interpersonal or organizational dynamics within the Attention-Deficit Workplace, but you can change how you respond within that environment. Remember that you are the CEO and president of your life and you're in charge of how you spend your time and attention.**

The 59th Lesson

✓ After reading many of the parables and lessons in *The Attention-Deficit Workplace*, you may notice several inherent contradictions. After all, it's surely poor karma to be a rising star in your own workplace while also turning a cold shoulder to obviously flawed colleagues. And though it's not your job to be 100 percent responsible for the behavior and actions of others, friendly advice can go a long way in helping those who lack the necessary business skills to be successful. For example, the hapless individual described in "The Incredible Shrinking Employee" (page 13) could have benefited if the company had provided him with a link to information about a communication workshop or personal development weekend before he was terminated.

Yet it's still important to know how best to avoid those people and obstacles standing in your way, so that you can have an open and uninhibited platform for loyal, honest interactions with co-workers and colleagues. First, you must start by placing a premium on your time. Be honest with others. Tell them when you're busy. Tell them when you don't have time for them. They will appreciate your candor.

By tightly guarding your time in the workplace, you are serving yourself and your company. It's a waste of everyone's time, attention, and energy to dance around critical matters like hidden agendas, lack of focus, and incompetence. If things aren't going right, be honest and direct with others. In the highly charged world of entrepreneurial ventures, truth and integrity are not prizes you accumulate like Boy Scout merit badges; they're good business.

On a recent trip to New York City, I met with Esther Dyson, the world-famous tech-sector guru and futurist who runs a conference called PC Forum (likely the very best tech conference). Over breakfast, I happened to describe to her the incident mentioned in the

"Pay Attention to the Details of Communication" parable (page 11) about the cheating girlfriend who was exposed through an e-mail ploy by her suspicious significant other. Esther's reaction should be enshrined in every workplace: "Wouldn't it just be easier if everyone simply told the truth?"

But telling the truth all the time is often difficult. Minor white lies permeate our daily lives, especially when we feel the need to protect someone else's feelings. Or when people engage in secretive "need-to-know" business relationships in the workplace, this can trigger all kinds of deception, not by outright lying but through factual omission. Deceit then grows into something much larger and more harmful. So nip it in the bud. Truth is the only lasting currency.

Everyone will ultimately know everything about one another in the electronic workplace, either through the enhanced human chain of information, e-mail forwards, Google, weblogs, or by a disgruntled techie who recovers the hard drive from your old computer and hacks into it. The electronic trail is transparent. It's smart to interact with others through this simple visualization: Imagine a handful of people looking over your shoulder as you type; they're watching. You don't know who they are, and you don't know if they are on your side or not; they are from the future, and they will someday see what you just typed.

You've likely heard your inner voice speaking when deciding if something is right or wrong. Well, listen to it. Pay attention to what it's saying. This applies to sending e-mails or talking to others. By always communicating the truth, whether it's by a BlackBerry, instant messenger, phone, or brief interactions in the hallway with your co-workers, you will find that people prefer to interact with those who maintain a strong moral code at all times.

Nothing threatens your time and attention more than integrity-deficit actions, and their resulting clean-up. Success in the workplace is a direct result of integrity. The headlines may go to the

Genghis Khan types who lop off the heads of their business rivals, but long-term profits will ultimately go to those who bring a decent and fair return to everyone involved. When you cut corners or when you undermine others for the sake of ego or profit, you are only hurting yourself.

Bottom Line: Always maintain your integrity. If you build every transaction and relationship in business and life with your behavior guided by the concepts of mutual benefit, fairness, and truth, the profits will come.

—ᘯᘯ—

ACKNOWLEDGMENTS

WHAT IS LIFE, if you are not surrounded by a support crew of family, friends, and associates? A very special thanks to Bill Katovsky, who is a major creative driving force behind this book—and other projects. To Tim Carlson for always being there to help. A heartfelt thanks to my mom, Lori Thrower, for her lifelong support and love. A bow of thanks to all the investors in the various ventures who have supported me through thick and thin, but especially to Ron Taylor at Enterprise Partners who believed in my idea for the participatory sports business model and took the leap of faith—after he made me stay up all night to write the vision statement for the company that became The Active Network, Inc.

To that very special team at Active, those currently still working, and to the team members who have worked there before and moved on. Without your effort, energy, and support, Active might have become In-active.com long ago. To the amazing Lisa Autenrieth, for believing in me through the tornado and helping to calm the winds. To Bob Stern, Todd Adelman, and Greg Smith for the early days of sweat and tears at our first company; to Mike Fuller, who purchased my first entrepreneurial venture. To David Wynam, Scott Kunkel, Dan Rivetti at the University of San Diego. To Adam Thornbrough, who inspired me to get off my crutches and start to run again; to Scott Dunklee, for his friendship and support. And, of course, to the high-energy Kristi Connell Nova. A heartfelt thanks to Frank Potenziani for sharing his perspective on the universe of human interaction, and for his efforts to change the world for the better. To Tom McCarthy and Jessie Shiers at The Lyons Press for giving this book the time and attention it deserves.

Appreciation goes to John Duke for his shameless shepherding over the *Triathlete* magazine. An Ironman "Mahalo" to Ben Fertic and Lew Friedland, at the World Triathlon Corporation. To Billy Gerber,

Wes Hein, Matt Barger, and Russ Crabs, for serving as the "super-friends" investor team. And to Steve Gintowt, the financial guru and the savior of all of my ventures—for taking the leap of faith, and for paying attention to the details of success. To Tom Hill, co-author of *Chicken Soup for the Entrepreneurial Soul*, for turbo-charging my commitment to write. To Steve Hansen for his friendship and advice. To Scott Kyle for his navigational skills on land and at sea. To Kimo Mc-Cormick at Allen Matkins in Orange County, for his strong support and hard work. To Andrew Lessman for his inspirational leadership and corporate excellence. To Craig Collins, the real-world Indiana Jones, whose advice always proves correct. To Wendy, who truly is all heart.

To Warren Buffett for his open expression of the secrets of his success. To the founding team of Active Europe: Laurent Gauthier, Eric Lyky, Jason Egnal, Bob Brown, Emily Primrose, Dominique Montaggioni, and Bruno Caviler. To Tai Yee and Paul Kiang for their unconditional support of my ventures. A very special thanks to the skilled technology professional, Cedric Mollet. To Joe Welch for showing everyone what a work ethic really is, and to the über-design king, Christian Riggs of the Riggs Creative Group. Reaching back in time, a heartfelt thanks to a very special coach named Pat Smith, who chiseled self-confidence and leadership into whatever raw material I had. To those three stars of Orion's belt, wherever you are . . .

Finally, to my sister Stacey, who died at the age of 16. During her brief time here, she taught me how to deal with real adversity and awakened within me the power of curiosity.